KETO *and* INTERMITTENT FASTING

The Most Exhaustive Guide for a
Rapid Weight Loss. Detox and Heal
Your Body with an Easy to Follow
30-Day Ketogenic Diet Meal Plan

MELISSA DREW
JORGE MOORE

Table of Contents

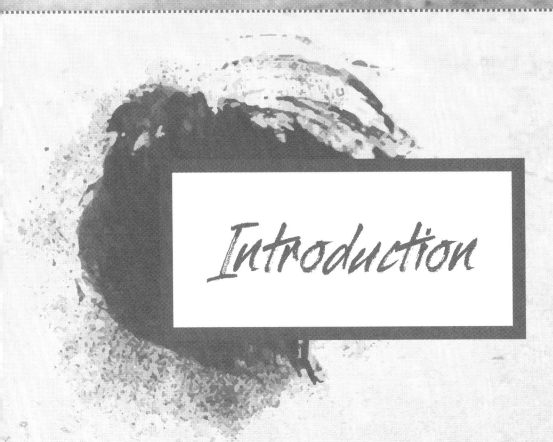

Introduction

Considering you are reading this book, it is safe to say that you want to shed off some extra pounds that you may have. You may not like your current appearance, want to fit in some clothes for a special occasion, or you just want to get healthy, whatever the case this is the right book for you. As weight loss is not a new issue, there have been various approaches to it. If you have been looking around for fast weight loss regiments, then there is a high chance that you have come across the words 'intermittent fasting' and 'ketogenic diet.'

The most generic advice that people give for weight loss is for you to eat a lot of whole-grain carbohydrates and to keep away from saturated fat as if it were taboo. Do you know that it is all a lie? Your body needs fat, and it is actually the main component of the ketogenic diet, and it contributes to most of the calories in the diet. You will learn more about this in later chapters.

Once you begin following the guidelines we explain further, you will shed those extra pounds in no time, feel healthier, and even look, fitter. And if you keep following them they will turn into a lifestyle.

Intermittent fasting can make you get a fair chance in the fight against excess fat. It has been used across the ages in different societies all around the world. It is even an integral part of many religions and cultures as it helps clear your mind and clear toxins that have accumulated in your body.

This approach to burn fat has gained a lot of popularity due to the ease in doing it and its effectiveness in burning fat. Movie stars, athletes, and even regular people use intermitting fasting to keep their weight under control. People, however, do not have a lot of information on how to correctly follow it, they have vague ideas, and this makes them come to false conclusions which are not backed up by facts.

Among the wrong ideas about the ketogenic diet and IF (Intermitting Fasting) the most common one is that they imply starvation. Starvation, by definition, is the lack of food which is not under the control of the individual. While fasting is a choice and it is a controlled lack of food, it is purely optional and has huge benefits, both physically and health-wise. Once you learn more about these approaches, they will become a 'must-have' in your life. Another false claim is that these methods of fasting will make you tired, weak, and slow your metabolic rate; these are all hogwash stories. As a side note, starvation is very dangerous; it can destroy your body and even prevent weight loss.

We as human are all different, the effect of these eating systems can vary from one person to another but with several modifications to them so that they can suit you, there will only be benefits. Unfortunately, there are some individuals who should not attempt these fat loss regiments. If you have any severe health issues, it is mandatory to seek medical advice prior to beginning the new lifestyle, even if you are generally healthy, it is still advisable to consult a professional.

To clarify things even before diving right into the pool of data contained in this book, it is best to understand the difference between IF and the keto diet. IF is not a diet, but a meal planner that is designed to enhance weight loss and other health advantages, the keto diet is a diet that highly restricts carbohydrates and increases the amount of fat that you take so that you can be fuller for longer and be able to make fat your main energy source in the midst of other advantages that will be discussed later on.

The main reason why many doctors and nutritional experts give the "calories in-calories out" advice is that on paper it is simple and direct. They think that excessive calorie intake is the main cause of obesity; thus, the direct way of reversing this is consuming fewer calories. The 'eat less and move more' approach has been done for a very long time, and it simply does not work. The reason is that obesity and excessive weight gain is more of a hormonal imbalance than a calories imbalance. You will learn more about this and how the IF and the ketogenic diet can assist you in correcting this.

By reading this book, you will find a vast amount of information about IF and the ketogenic diet. You will know why and how they work so well and how they can work together to enhance your weight loss experience. You will also know about their benefits and downsides and how to be safe as you practice them.

DISCLAIMER: this book is for educational and information purposes only and it is not a substitute for professional consultation or advice. **You should always consult a medical professional, to be able to modify this information to suit him/her where required.** It is your choice to follow the data located in this book or not since your life is in your hands. Thank you and enjoy.

Chapter 1

Why Do We Gain Weight

In order to be prepared to lose weight correctly, you must first know why you gain it. Lack of sufficient exercise and having too much to eat are not enough reasons to explain this occurrence; it would be the same as saying that anyone who doesn't get all A's in class just doesn't read enough; there are many other reasons behind it. Usually, the final result is the ultimate judge of what is the best way to deal with excessive weight, and you will come to see that the best combination is IF and the ketogenic diet. It is impossible to dispute the facts.

Over the years, individuals in the weight loss society have become familiar and trusted in the sentence 'calories in, calories out.' This makes it appear that consuming fewer calories will result in equal fat burning, it may seem very reasonable, but does it actually work?

Obesity levels over the years have skyrocketed, even though everywhere in the world the dieting advice is to reduce calories, is it a coincidence? You might think that those who were given this advice were not able to correctly follow it, but have you ever regarded the chance that altogether this advice might be incorrect?

Several trials have been carried out in order to test this approach of slimming down, and the findings will make you speechless. The average rate of success was only 3 percent, which means that the rate of failure was 97 percent. This is not the result of one study but of many researches conducted over years in different locations, as you can see it seems the error levels are extremely large. Not only did these people eat less, but they also exercised, nevertheless there was no significant change in their results even after a lot of exercising. This approach simply doesn't work, and even if you're fortunate enough to be among the 3 percent, you're going to get back the fat lost even quicker than it took you to get rid of it. The evidence is in the outcomes, and it has proved ineffective in this strategy.

Many individuals have a fake perception of calories that leads them to think this strategy "calorie in, calories out" is the only one. They believe they're all packed up and placed in one location where the body receives them and uses them when you need them, usually when you move or exercise. They also believe that all types of calories deposits, glucose, and glycogen, are equivalent while they are very distinct.

The body puts away energy for subsequent use in the liver and in body fat. It is important to know that your system gets power from fat, sugar, and even proteins (they are essential). Your system though cannot store surplus proteins, thus it transforms them into glucose that is deposited in the liver as glycogen. Once the glycogen shops in the liver are filled, excess calories are collected as body fat.

Think of glycogen as a refrigerator and body fat as a cold room to better comprehend the distinction between the two. Refrigerators are the best for short-term food storage because they are readily available but have a finite ability. Cold spaces are not readily available, but they compensate for this because they have very big storage capacity and are therefore best suited for long-term food storage. Once the refrigerator is full, items are transferred to the cold room so that more space can be created. The refrigerator's availability increases the chance that you will get meals from there rather than from cold rooms. These are the same rules used by your body. Prior to using body fat, your body uses glycogen present in the liver to get energies. In order to enable your body to use fat, you are required to finish all the glycogen as your body cannot get energy from fat and glucose simultaneously.

Different variables lead to weight gains, such as snacking between meals, insufficient sleep, stress, and insufficient practice, among others. When individuals snack between meals they most probably eat junk food that's just sophisticated carbohydrates, they're addictive, full of calories, and they influence your insulin concentrations.

White rice, junk food, bread, and many more have highly digestible carbohydrates that quickly break down and result in instant energy in the bloodstream. Too much blood sugar can damage your dangerous nerves and blood vessels.

Your pancreas will produce large quantities of insulin to restore your blood sugar concentrations to normal. If you regularly eat meals and do nothing to burn the surplus calories, your sensitivity to insulin is supposed to decrease. The more you snack, the more insulin is produced, leading to an inflammation of your fat cells as a lot of energy is trying to get jammed into them. The fullness of your fat cells will result in a fat overflow. The constantly elevated concentrations of insulin will make you feel starving, even as you store a bunch of fat in your framework. Your body won't be able to use stored energy, but instead is going to push you to eat more energy food. Your weight issue can be caused by elevated concentrations of insulin in your blood.

Our bodies, likewise many other living organisms, were naturally created to adapt to modifications. At first, the use of painkillers for things like headaches is efficient, but ultimately your body will stop being sensitive to the drugs making it necessary to take more to get the same impact you've had from getting a little. This is the same thing that occurs when you have elevated levels of insulin in your blood; it takes more to have the same impact as before. Correcting enhanced painkiller strength by decreasing the number and quantity of medicines given is the same as correcting insulin resistance.

Constant production of high insulin amounts puts you at more risk than just gaining weight. You may also be subject to cancer of the intestine and breast, high blood pressure, dementia, acne, uneven cycles, mood changes, infertility, and development of excess hair. Your insulin concentrations eventually determine your body's ease of access to body fat. Even if your system has some small insulin concentrations of glucose, it can prevent you to consume body fat. Your body can consume more easily body fat when your glycogen concentrations are small.

Besides enabling access to small insulin concentrations of fat shops, it also causes energy fat burning. You think you should have very low insulin levels to get the most effortless fat burning experience, but that's not the case. Irregularly small insulin concentrations trigger continuous burning of fat, making it difficult for you to store fat regardless of the number of calories consumed. This is what is called type 1 diabetes and may cause death if left untreated. In order to allow the body to store fat, people affected by this illness are provided with insulin injections.

You should first pass through stored glycogen to burn body fat for energy. When your glycogen concentrations are small, you feel starving, so you want to eat more. Your metabolism is reduced if you have elevated concentrations of insulin, but your glycogen shops are not full. This doesn't make you burn fat even if you don't eat. High concentrations of insulin can hamper your attempts to lose fat. As a survival mechanism, when glycogen or nutrition is accessible, your body will not use body fat to guarantee that body fat will be present in moments of need. Because your fat shops are not drained throughout the day, continuous consumption makes it harder to access fat shops.

The result of changing the workplace is a response. Your body doesn't want to modify its weight, so it's going to attempt to get back to that weight. Your body attempts to make you recover your weight when you lose weight by making you feel more hungry. This is the consequence of fat storage being inaccessible as the concentrations of insulin are large. Your metabolism will be slowed down, as mentioned previously, thus showing the effect of insulin on weight loss. This is why you will encounter weight loss plateaus and weight recovery by following some diets. That's what happens when you use the "eat less to get the weight you want" technique.

If you practice excessively and are unable to keep the pace for a long period and decrease the quantity, your metabolism will slow down so you will experience a plateau in weight loss. Keeping on going with the same diet will lead to weight gain after your body lowers the number of calories it needs to operate and adjusts to the new regime.

Increasing the quantity of accessible junk food also performs a role in weight gain. These processed foods are very inexpensive and easily accessible. Many products are marketed as fat-free, making individuals believe they're healthier and use them to replace extremely digestible carbohydrates while they are effectively worse.

If you are allergic to a certain sort of foodstuff, you may have more fat in your body. Food is addictive, but not as addictive as hard drugs. There is a certain sort of enjoyment that comes from eating some products, even though we understand they're not safe. An instance of an addictive food is chocolate and other sugar products; you may want to consume them not because you're starving, but simply because you like them. Using the Keto diet and IF, this addiction can be lowered and ultimately eradicated.

Snacking between meals also increases weight gain. Snacking between meals has become the norm over the years, which was previously not the situation. People would remain without meals for about five hours, but now individuals only remain for about three hours without snacking. People have been made to think that snacking will prevent you from eating a big dinner which is considered to be the source of fat gain. As a result, individuals only get more calories from snacking than from eating fat.

Low carbohydrate diets help to lower your insulin concentrations, but they aren't a hundred percent efficient as proteins increase insulin concentrations, so fasting helps as everything is limited, so nothing peaks your insulin levels. Very low carbohydrate diets can best assist people with type 2 diabetes, as blood sugar concentrations are reduced. It gives you a bunch of fasting impacts without any fasting at all. Fasting is stronger, but the mixture of the two can lead to the biggest consequence.

Intermittent fasting can also reverse insulin resistance while reducing your calorie consumption. By regularly eating, although it takes fewer calories, the same fasting hormonal modifications are not possible. IF stabilizes or even boost your metabolism when fasting while diets reduce metabolism. Growth hormone and adrenaline are generated as the body transit from burning sugar to burning fat to maintaining energy and muscle mass as insulin and blood sugar decline. Fat burning levels may be similar, but insulin levels are significantly different. A study was performed to see the difference between the two methods. After the same period of time, both sample groups had about the same weight and weight loss.

The caloric reduction has a problem with high insulin levels and eventually, higher insulin resistance that can add to obesity. This problem cannot be decreased by insulin resistance, which eventually contributes to weight regeneration, not only for very small carbohydrate diets but also for other diets. Fasting generates long periods of low insulin levels that prevent elevated insulin and insulin resistance. Most of these diets do not take into consideration the reality that the body adapts to changing circumstances; this is called homeostasis. Continuous reduced calorie intake will assist the body to adapt to it in order to stop weight loss. Intermittent fasting and Ketogenic diet are perfect because they are not constant, so the body cannot adapt to them to avoid weight loss.

The Ketogenic diet can bring you in a state of ketosis, just like full hunger, but it's safer. This is because there is a lot of protein loss from muscle cells during full hunger while in the Ketogenic diet body mass is maintained. Most of the weight wasted during full hunger consists of muscle mass and water and this is wrong. Although protein loss decreases as you go on, it's still not nice. The Ketogenic diet was created to allow individuals to benefit from full hunger without the health consequences of hunger such as ketosis, repression of appetite, and energy dependence on body fat and ketones. All this is going to be discussed in this book further.

Some medical procedures can help you achieve the same fasting effects, one of this is bariatric surgery. This procedures includes the surgical removal of your stomach. It can lower your blood pressure and curb weight restoration. Various people think that once part of the stomach is cut off, there is less hormone production as the stomach produces many hormones; but this is not how it works. Gastric banding proved that this assumption is wrong. In fact, instead of removing a part of the stomach it consists of pressing a band around the stomach to make it smaller, and it has the same effects as the bariatric surgery, so the hormone decline hypothesis is incorrect. There are other methods accessible to reduce fat, such as liposuction, which blows out the fat but it only has cosmetic benefits, and no metabolic benefits.

The problem is why would you choose to go through these expensive processes that can contribute to some problems while you can exercise IF. IF and Keto diet should be a breeze for you allowing you to avoid adverse effects such as injuries associated with surgery. IF and Keto diet is the best and cheapest method to burn fat and correct hormone imbalances.

Keto and
Intermittent Fasting

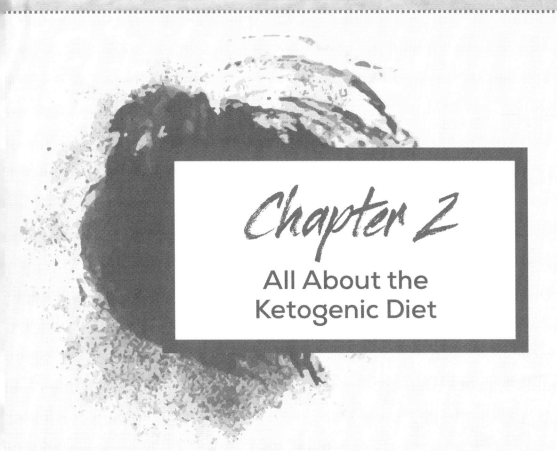

Chapter 2

All About the Ketogenic Diet

What is the ketogenic diet?

A diet that results in the production of ketone bodies from the liver is referred to as a ketogenic diet; it makes your system utilize fat over carbs for energy. It limits the intake of carbs to a low level causing some reactions. It's not a towering protein diet, though. It involves moderate protein, low carbs, and high-fat consumption. The precise percentage of macronutrients will vary depending on your requirements. Fat makes up to 75 percent of the calories you ingest thus is a fundamental component of the diet, proteins occupy 20% of the calories you take, and carbs make up to 5%.

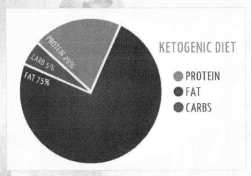

KETOGENIC DIET

- PROTEIN
- FAT
- CARBS

Your system usually works with a mixture of proteins, carbs, and fats. This diet removes carbohydrates, causing your system's stores to become depleted and the body finds an alternative source of power. Many of your organs can use free fatty acids, but not all of them can use ketone bodies, for instance, the brain and nervous system they can't, however use ketone bodies.

Insufficient free fatty acid disintegration releases ketone bodies as by-product. The power supplied is fat non-carbohydrate obtained which is used by organs like the brain. As a consequence of ketone bodies rapid processing, which makes them accumulate in the blood, our body develops ketosis. The use and processing of glucose in your system is also reduced; so it is also reduced the protein used for energy.

The levels of glucagon and glucose are affected by ketogenic diets. Insulin transforms glucose into glycogen that is recycled as fat while glucagon transforms glycogen into glucose to provide your system with energy. Carbs removal from the diet improves the levels of glucagon and decreases levels of insulin. This, in the end, causes liberation of an increased number of FFA and their decomposition in the liver that results in the processing of ketone bodies and induces the ketosis state.

The diet is, in a way identical to starvation with the distinction being that in this diet food is eaten. The metabolic impacts that come about and the adjustments experienced in starvation are approximately the same as those experienced during this diet. There has been an extensive study of the reaction to complete hunger, probably more so than the diet on its own. That's why the vast bulk of information described is derived from the analyses of fasting individuals. There are few exceptions, but the diet's metabolic impacts are similar to those that occur during starvation. The reactions in ketosis as a result of carb restriction are the same as the reactions seen with starvation. In this regard, protein and fat amounts are not that important.

Considering how carbs are not wanted in this diet, it may leave you wondering how much is needed for daily sustenance by your system. The body undergoes at least three significant adjustments when carbs are taken away from the diet to preserve the little glucose and protein it has. The principal adjustment is a general change in energy source to FFA from glucose in most of your organs. This change spares the slight quantity of glucose accessible to fuel the brain. In the leukocytes, erythrocytes, and bone marrow that continue to use glucose, the second adaptation happens. These tissues break down glucose partly to lactate and pyruvate that go to the liver and are transferred back to glucose to avoid the depletion of accessible glucose reserve. Therefore, this issue doesn't end in a large decrease of glucose in your system and can be ignored in terms of the carbs need of the body. The third, and likely the most important, adjustment happens in your body, which, by the third week of continuous ketosis, transforms to the use of ketones for 75% of the power demands instead of getting from carbs. Since the brain continuously depletes glucose in the body, the regular carbohydrate demands are all that we need to bother ourselves with.

Your brain uses about 100 g of glucose daily in regular conditions. This implies that any diet that is based on fewer than 100 g of carbs daily will cause ketosis, the level of which depends on how many carbs are consumed that is to say: the fewer carbs eaten, the greater the ketosis. Eating carbs below 100 grams will result in ketosis. With the continued adaptation of the brain to the use of ketones for energy and the glucose demands of your system declining, fewer carbs should be absorbed so as to sustain the ketosis state.

There is no one-size-fits-all when it comes with how much of your total calorie requirement you should derive from carbs. Some nutritionist advice that people to keep it in the low end, which is five percent but it is not necessarily good advice as the exact amount depends on your system. To get the right amount for you, you will have to rely on the trial and error method. Select a percentage and see how it feels for you if you don't like the results you can adjust accordingly. With fats and protein, just like in carbs, there is no exact amount for everyone. It all depends on you, but seventy-five percent is a good place to start off.

There is no space to "cheat" on your diet here. You should follow it completely as even one meal that does not follow its rules can slow down your advancement for about a week as your body is withdrawn from ketosis. Always make sure you've eaten enough so that you will not be tempted to have a snack that could ruin all you've been working for so far.

Macronutrients and ketosis

Proteins, carbs, and fats are the three macronutrients. Because of their effect on glucose in the blood and hormone concentrations, all three nutrients have different impacts on ketosis. Because of its impacts on blood sugar and insulin (increasing both), carbohydrate is 100% anti-ketogenic. Protein roughly is more anti-ketogenic than ketogenic since more than half of the protein ingested is transformed into sugar and insulin is increased. Fat is more ketogenic than anti-ketogenic, its anti-ketogenic property is as a result of the tiny transformation of triglyceride glycerol to sugar. Although alcohol has no immediate impact on ketosis, excessive consumption of alcohol can lead to ketoacidosis.

Before debating how to avoid loss of nitrogen during hunger, we need to describe the impacts of various nutrients on ketosis. Both the intake of carbs and protein will affect the development of ketosis, influencing the changes seen, and also how much of the effect of "protein sparing" will happen. Even if the nature of this diet is at "elevated fat" levels, or at least this is how it is viewed, dietary fat intake has a minimal impact on ketosis per se. The primary effect of fat ingestion is the amount of it that is burned for energy. Alcohol's implementation of ketogenic diets is somewhat restricted.

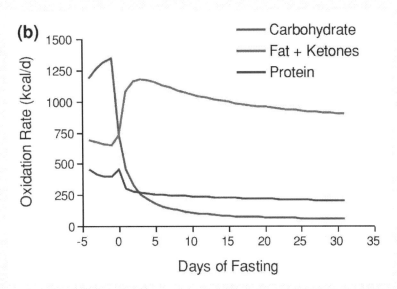

The equation used to create ketogenic diets for epileptic infants reflects the comparative inclination of a specified macronutrient to either support a ketogenic state or stop it. By now, you must have realized that the key players in deciding the change of a ketogenic state are glycogen and glucose, this equation reflects fundamentally the inclination of a specified nutrient to elevate glucose or glycogen. This typically results in a 4-gram fat diet for every 1 g of carbs or proteins; it is referred to as a 4:1 diet. While this percentage is critically crucial in clinical environments for implementing the diet, we see in that it is not as essential to the overall dieting public.

Carbs are a 100% anti-ketogenic. They enter the blood glucose in the form of glucose after digestion, increasing insulin, and reducing glucagon, which inhibits the development of ketone bodies. As noted in the past section, only the brain requires approximately 100 g of glucose daily. If enough carbs are eaten to provide that much glucose, there is no need for the brain to start running on ketones. A diet that causes a blood sugar increase or has over 100 g of carbs daily is not ketogenic. The brain's glucose demands will fall to about 40 g daily in 3 weeks, or so thus you must further limit your carbs. In addition, the more carbs are reduced within the first few days of starting the diet, resulting in fast depletion of liver glycogen, the quicker you will get in the ketosis state and the higher its level.

Impacts caused by proteins is partially in favour and partially against the diet. This is as a result of 58% of proteins getting in the blood as glucose, thus causing insulin levels to rise and prevent ketosis. The insulin reaction to protein is quite small as compared to carbs. Protein must, therefore, be limited to some extent as too much will produce a lot of glucose which can impair or prevent ketosis. Protein also triggers the processing of glucagon and has some impacts that are pro-ketogenic. Protein intake's most critical element has to do with stopping body protein disintegration. The breakdown of protein can be reduced or completely prevented by offering dietary protein during hunger. Fat mainly affects ketogenic positively but has a small negative impact. This is seen as 10% of the complete eaten fat will appear as water in the bloodstream. If 180 grams of fat is burned daily, the transformation of glycerol will provide 18 grams of glucose.

Even if alcohol isn't depicted in the equation and has no immediate effect on ketosis, the intake of alcohol will affect the strength of ketosis and the quantity of fat that your system utilizes. Excessive consumption of alcohol during ketosis may lead to the development of runaway acidosis that is possibly very hazardous. On top of limiting the amount of FFA that can be handled by the liver, alcohol calories will detract from the general fat burning. The reality is that a ketogenic diet's initial decrease in weight is due to water loss. The issue is if a ketogenic diet loses more or less real weight as compared to other diets.

Most studies have shown a greater weight loss in low-carb diets as opposed to high-carb diets, but this is not always the case. The level of fat-burning observed is usually the same for ketogenic versus non-ketogenic diets once the water has been considered. That is, if

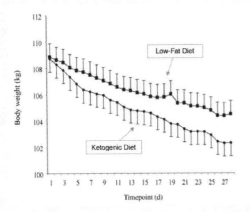

individuals are placed on a diet of 1200 calories daily, there will be an equal amount of weight loss no matter the diet. Weight loss is not a diet's primary objective. Rather, the objective is to maximize fat loss with muscle loss minimization.

The fundamental assumption of the diet is that increased fat and less protein are needed to create the specified caloric deficit by promoting fat use over the rest. It stands out that the diet with the highest nitrogen balance as a result, has the biggest fat loss. Unfortunately, the absence of well-conducted research makes it hard to sustain this assumption.

Benefits and downsides of Ketogenic diet

Nothing is perfect; the Ketogenic diet is no exception. It has many benefits and some downsides. Some of the benefits include:

Reduction of cravings and appetite

Many people gain weight simply because they can't control their cravings and appetites of calorie-filled foods. The Ketogenic diet helps to eradicate these problems, but it doesn't mean that you will never become hungry or not desire to eat food at all. You will feel hungry but only when you need to eat. Several studies have shown that fewer amounts of carbohydrates you eat, the less you generally eat. Eating healthier high-fat foods help to stop your large appetite. According to several studies, more weight is lost faster on a low carb rather than a low-fat diet. This is because low carb diets help you lose more water from your body and lower insulin levels as your body does not need a very high amount of insulin to turn glycogen into glucose. This diet helps you to eliminate visceral fat; thus, you will acquire a slimmer appearance and shape. It is the most difficult fat to lose as it surrounds your organs as it gets more. High amounts of it can cause inflammation and insulin resistance. Coconut oil can produce an instant source of energy as it boosts ketone levels in your body.

Reduction of risk of heart disease

Triglycerides, fat molecules in your body, have close links with heart disease. They are directly proportional as the more the number of triglycerides, the higher your chances of suffering from heart disease. You can reduce the number of free triglycerides in your body by reducing the number of carbohydrates as it is in the keto diets.

Reduces chances of having high blood pressure

Weight loss and blood pressure have a close connection; thus, since you are losing weight while on the keto diet, it will affect your blood pressure.

Fights type 2 diabetes

Type two diabetes develops as a result of insulin resistance. This is a result of having huge amounts of glucose in your system, with the keto diet this is not a possibility due to the low carbohydrate intake.

Increases the production of HDL

High-density lipoprotein is referred to as good cholesterol. It is responsible for caring calories to your liver, thus they can be reused. High fat and low carbohydrate diets increase the production of HDL in your body, which also reduces your chances of getting a heart disease. Low-density lipoprotein is referred to as bad cholesterol.

Suppresses your appetite

It is a strange but true effect of the keto diet. It was thought that this was as a result of the production of ketones, but this was proven wrong as a study taken between people on a regular balanced diet and some on the keto diet showed their appetites were generally the same. It helps to suppress appetite as it has a higher fat content than many other diets. Food stays in the stomach for longer as fat is digested slowly, thus providing a sense of fullness for a longer time. On top of that, proteins promote the secretion cholecystokinin, which is a hormone that contributes in regulating appetite. It is also believed that the ketogenic diet helps to suppress your appetite by continuously blunting it. There is increased appetite in the initial stages of the diet, which decreases over time.

Changes in cholesterol levels

This is kind of on the fence between good and bad. This is because the ketogenic diet involves a high fat intake which makes people wonder about the effect on blood lipids and its potential to increase chances of heart disease and strokes, among others. Several major components play a lead role in determining this, which is: LDL, HDL, and blood triglyceride levels. Heart disease correlates with high levels of LDL and cholesterol. On the other hand, high levels of HDL are seen as protection from diseases caused by cholesterol levels. The impacts of the diet on cholesterol are not properly known. Some research has shown that there is no change in cholesterol levels while others have said that there is change. If you stay in deep ketosis for a very long period of time, your blood lipids will increase, but you will have to go through some negative effects of the ketogenic diet which will be corrected when the diet is over. If a person does not remain following the diet strictly for like ten years, he/she will not experience any cholesterol problems. It is difficult to differentiate between diet and weight loss in general. The effect of the ketogenic diet on cholesterol has been boiled down to if you lose fat on the ketogenic diet then your cholesterol levels will go down, and if you don't lose fat, then your cholesterol levels will go up. Strangely, women have a larger cholesterol level addition than men, while both are on a diet. As there is no absolute conclusion on the effect of the ketogenic diet on cholesterol, you are advised to have your blood lipid levels constantly checked for any bad effects. Blood lipid levels should be checked before starting the diet and about eight weeks after starting. If repeated results show a worsening of lipid levels, then you should abandon the diet or substitute saturated fats with unsaturated fats.

The ketogenic diet also has some downsides, which include:

Low energy levels

When available, the body prefers to use carbohydrates for fuel as they burn more effectively than fats. General drop-in energy level is a concern raised by many dieters due to the lack of carbohydrates. Studies have shown that it causes orthostatic hypotension which causes lightheadedness. It has come to be known that these effects can be avoided by providing enough supplemental nutrients like sodium. Many of the symptoms can be prevented by providing 5 grams of sodium per day. Most times, fatigue disappears after a few weeks or even days, if fatigue doesn't disappear, then you should add a small number of carbohydrates to the diet as long as ketosis is maintained. The diet is not recommended when caring out high-intensity workouts, weight training, or high-intensity aerobic exercise as carbohydrates are an absolute requirement but are okay for low-intensity exercise.

Effects on the brain

It causes increased use of ketones by the brain. The increased use of ketones, among other reasons, result in the treating of childhood epilepsy. As a result of the changes that occur, the concern over the side effects, including permanent brain damage and short term memory loss, has been raised. The origin of these concerns is difficult to understand. The brain is powered by ketones in the absence of glucose. Ketones are normal energy sources and not toxic as the brain creates enzymes, during fetal growth, that helps us use them. Epileptic children, though not the perfect examples, show some insight into the effects of the diet on the brain in the long term. There is no negative effect in terms of cognitive function. There is no assurance that the diet cannot have long term dietary effects, but no information proves that there are any negative effects. Some people feel they can concentrate more when on the ketogenic diet, while others feel nothing but fatigue. This is as a result of differences in individual physiology. There are very few studies that vaguely address the point on short term memory loss. This wore off with the continuation of the study.

Kidney stones and kidney damage

As a result of the increased workload from having to filter ketones, urea, and ammonia, as well as dehydration concerns of the potential for kidney damage or passing kidney stones have been raised. The high protein nature of the ketogenic diet raises the alarms of individuals who are concerned with potential kidney damage. There is very little information that points to any negative effects of the diet on kidney function or development of kidney stones. There is a low incidence of small kidney stones in epileptic children this may be as a result of the state of deliberate dehydration that the children are put at instead of the ketosis state itself. Some short term research shows no change in kidney function or increased incidents of kidney stones either after they are off the diet or after six months on a diet. There is no long term data on the effects of ketosis to kidney function; thus, no complete conclusions can be made. People with preexisting kidney issues are the only ones who get problems from high protein intake. From an unscientific point of view, one would expect increased incidents of this to happen to athletes who consume very high protein diets, but it has not happened. This suggests that high protein intake, under normal conditions, is not harmful to the kidneys. To limit the possibility of kidney stones, it is advised to drink a lot of water to maintain hydration. People who are predisposed to kidney stones should have their kidney function monitored to ensure that no complications arise if they decide to follow the diet.

Constipation

A common side effect of the diet is reduced bowel movements and constipation. This arises from two different causes: lack of fiber and gastrointestinal absorption of foods. First, the lack of carbs in the diet means that unless supplements are taken, fiber intake is low. Fiber is very important to our systems. High fiber intake can prevent some health conditions, including heart disease and some forms of cancer. Use some type of sugar-free fiber supplement to prevent any health problems and help you maintain regular bowel movements. The diet also reduces the volume of stool due to enhanced absorption and digestion of food; thus, fewer waste products are generated.

Fat regain

Dieting, in general, has very low long-term success rates. There are some effects of getting out of a ketogenic diet like the regain of fat lost through calorific restriction alone. This is true for any diet based on calorific restriction. It is expected for weight to be regained after carb reintroduction. For people who use the weighing scale to measure their success, they may completely shun carbs as they think it is the main reason for the weight regain. You should understand that most of the initial weight gain is water and glycogen.

Immune system

There is a large variety in the immunity system response to ketogenic diets on different people. There has been some repost on reduction on some ailments such allergies and increased minor sickness susceptibility.

Optic neuropathy

This is optic nerve dysfunction. It has appeared in a few cases. It was linked to the people not getting adequate amounts of calcium or vitamins supplements for about a year. All the cases were corrected by supplementation of adequate vitamin B, especially thiamine.

Chapter 3

All About
Intermittent Fasting

What is intermittent fasting?

Intermittent fasting is fasting at times when you keep away any kind of foodstuff involving calories among ordinary nutritious ingredients. It is not starvation or a way for you to eat junk food with no consequences. There are various methods used to practice IF, they either divide time into hours or divide time into days. Since the response of the regiment varies from person to person, no method can be called the best.

Knowing that intermittent fasting cannot make you lose the additional pounds you may have instantaneously is essential, but it can assist you to prevent unhealthy addictions to meals. It's a nutritional practice that requires you to be determined to follow in order to get the maximum gain. If you already have a minimum duration to eat due to your schedule, this regiment will suit you like a duck to water, but you will always need to be conscious of what you are eating if you are a foodie. Choose the appropriate regiment after expert guidance. You should see it as a segment of your schedule to get healthy, but not the only component.

If you do it frequently, your body becomes used to it; thus, it automatically becomes a regular practice for you. Your body will alter your hunger patterns, as you'll feel famished when you're ready to eat rather than false after hunger signals. It ends in quicker results when intermittent fasting is done for longer periods, but long fasts should be done less frequently. It is possible to switch plans, but don't do it because you find it hard at the beginning, as all of them are quite similar when it comes to that the more you do, the simpler it becomes.

Hormones that increase appetite and fat retention like insulin are influenced by your eating patterns. The number and time of eating affect your circadian rhythms. These circadian rhythms are predictable recurrent variations of hormone levels over a day — nearly all hormones, like those required for growth, secreted in a circadian rhythm.

The circadian rhythms are affected by the season and daytime. Food was most likely available during the day in the paleolithic period as they used the sunlight for hunting because at night they had no light source. Other animals have inverted circadian rhythms because at night they hunt and sleep in the day. You may consume the same meals, but the timing can create a large variation in your body's and general wellness. In the evening, the levels of insulin are higher than in the morning, so eating large meals can cause more fat being stored in your body. This helps connect the relationship between eating and obesity since it is more of a hormonal inequality than calorific inequality.

If you are in a heavily stressed environment, intermittent fasting can be hard. It can do the opposite of what you intended to do as it can increase fat storage. You should be conscious of why you are doing this and how otherwise it will produce more negative than beneficial results.

Believe it or not, a circadian rhythm is followed by hunger; otherwise, we would be hungry all the time. Hunger is lowest in the morning, and hunger is at its highest at night. Hormones affect when you feel hungry,so t he period you have stayed without eating doesn't matter. It takes time for your hormones to adjust so that during the first few days of fasting, you may feel hungry, but after that, you will not feel hungry during your time of fasting.

Many people say that breakfast is supposed to be the largest meal of the day, but in fact, you're the least hungry in the morning, as stated earlier. Eating a large breakfast is just forcing the body to eat food that it doesn't need; it has an adverse effect on your weight loss goals. Your insulin concentrations are highest at night, leading in a lot of conversion of glucose into fat; thus, more fat is stored when you eat a large meal in the evening. Lunchtime is the optimum time to eat the largest meal of the day.

During a diet, burning up stored fats is the way the body gets energy. This will teach your body to use fats for energy and to forfeit glucose even when you're not fasting. In locations like the heart and lungs, your body utilizes stored fat for energy, but more is generated as a consequence of unnecessary eating, replacing the fat used. Also, organs using recycled fat do not have enough time to use it as glucose is constantly carried into the system making them avoid using that fat, so the body first needs to get rid of it. If you eat a lot and do not exercise, the stored fat cannot be burned by your body cells.

By default, the cells of a healthy person are designed to burn fat for energy, so intermittent fasting is like adding gasoline to a fire. Encouraging your system to make fat your only energy source will help you lose more fat in the long run. Exercise can help you in this process. Exercise allows your cells to consume fat and glucose when the body needs it, providing you energy rather than enhancing fat retention.

Intermittent fasting enables you to discover a variety of things: you realize that hunger eventually stops and it doesn't make you eat excess food. These are myths that do not have strong proof but are based on notions of those who have never tried it. You will understand the reality once you search for yourself. You're going to improve as the body obviously adjusts to IF. Intermittent fasting can assist you to remain lean, keep your weight loss path secure, and keep your fresh shape running.

While IF is amazing, it cannot be done by everyone. This is particularly true for pregnant females and those who are still nursing their kids. These individuals need a high-calorie intake, which does not make IF a viable option. However, it can get your body back after you get the baby and finished nursing. Even if there is some proof that it can help with insulin imbalance and insensitivity, people with type 2 diabetes should not attempt this regiment. You shouldn't attempt the fasting regiment if you have a record of eating diseases or think you may get one. If you are looking for a weight loss scheme, but you are under 18 years of age, you should seek adequate guidance from a pediatrician because you should not attempt intermittent fasting.

Intermittent fasting is for those who want to regulate their hormones and burn surplus body fat. This diet allows healthier whole foods and an all-round diet which is better than living off processed foods and sugars which are unhealthy. It can also benefit individuals who are sugar-addicted or those who ate empty calories. Drinks and sodas with very few nutrients, but full of calories, are included in these products. Finally, people generally want to do better in life and want a food plan that doesn't require too much planning or maintenance. If you fall into one of those categories, this plan is for you. Even if intermittent fasting may not be for you reading this book will equip you with the necessary information required to help another person or to use it later in life.

Intermittent fasting rules

In order to attain a balance in almost every aspect of existence, rules must be put in place; the same applies to intermittent fasting. What time you eat, and the amount is determined by the level of activity you have each day. In days of hard work or exercise, carbohydrate consumption is higher than other nutrients. Foods high in good fats on relaxing days should be sky high above the others, while protein consumption should be constant regardless of the day. When your calorie intake is below normal consumption, weight loss occurs, generating a calorie deficit.

Many people don't know precisely what they want to lose when cutting down their size, but others know that they want to burn fat. Unfortunately, there is a hand in hand loss of fat and muscle that many don't want. As a result of daily consumption calorie reduction, your body reduces the muscles to regulate the number of calories used.

Our bodies and the Paleolithic man's body are on very different levels. To find shelter, they had to hunt and move continually, so their muscles were constantly put to work. We, the regular people of our time, are basically couch potatoes and have no excuse to use muscles. You can give your body a reason to maintain your muscle mass instead of letting it go by doing daily physical exercise, thus decreasing the amount of fat in your body. You can also avoid muscle loss by reducing your calorie demands gradually to prevent your energy demands from completing your fat deposits. This allows the body to adjust without effort to the new calorie limit. You can do this only because we all have different requirements for calories. A well-balanced combination of nutrients is a great way to obtain calories. Your daily calorific specifications are determined by the form, age, sex, and health status of your activity. Another way to calculate your calories is to check your weight and count the number of calories that you carry in a day for several periods.

Calories are calories wherever they are obtained. In the context of calories, there is no incorrect or correct food; it is only the calorific content of the food that matters. Within the same time duration, you can eat the same amount of different food types and end up gaining weight while taking one and losing weight when taking the other.

Far from calories, yes, food can be classified as right or wrong. Some will slowly but surely destroy you, while others will give your body tremendous benefits. These poor foodstuffs include processed products packed with so many additives, preservatives, and dye which can damage you by consuming them. Try to keep consuming these products at a minimal level or stop consuming them completely. It is best to eat organic foods that have undergone minimal or no treatment to protect your health. This day and age may seem hard, but it's possible. By gradually integrating organic foods into your periodic meals and avoiding processed foods, it can be accomplished, and ultimately you will become fully accustomed to it.

You must understand the distinction between hunger and starvation. The tremendous urge to eat any food around you shouldn't put an end to your fast just because there are small rambles in your belly. You feel hungry, but you're not supposed to succumb to the feeling. To avoid sensation, simply get it off your mind and focus on other things. You won't die as your body is made to last even longer without food. When you fast your metabolic rate remains the same, so your body system generally works, your metabolic rate begins to slow down after 72 hours, and there is no continuous program of fasting going to such extremes.

The little growling of your stomach is no problem, but abdominal pain is a problem. This is more than hunger, and instant medical assistance should be pursued. Hunger is a bodily reaction at the regular time it is used to. This happens in intermittent fasting, but hunger goes away after a while. To adjust the body to the new practice, you have to control yourself. Your mind is controlling your body, so don't let your body control you.

During your fast, you should take enough fluids. Weight loss and water loss go hand in hand, so you might get dehydrated if you're not cautious. Mostly we're too busy thinking about not consuming food that our minds forget about drinking water. Hydration is a very important part of any fast since you will feel awful if you don't get enough water. While it has the same benefits as regular water, carbonated water can help add more excitement.

Another great fasting drink is herbal teas which are produced from dried flowers and herb leaves, so there is no caffeine. Its good hydration and you can have as much as you like. Always read the recipes for components containing sweeteners or calories when purchasing these herbal teas. Black tea, a fermented tea, purple tea, and coffee can also be consumed.

Another drink for rehydration is bone broth. It also provides minerals, amino acids, and electrolytes. It can even make you feel less hungry with smell and taste. However, it tells the sensors of nutrients to tell the body that you are no longer in a fasted state, leading to a slight rise in insulin levels. It allows you to stay in a fast for longer, so it is equal to the transition of good and bad. For fasts that last longer than a day, the broth is better, leaving you hydrated and giving you a dose of minerals.

When breaking your fast, do it with a small lunch instead of a big one after the fasting period is over to check your comfort. You may not immediately have room for plenty of dishes. You can break a fast for a day or less with a small dinner. If the fast is for several days, you have to restart eating slowly by eating something light that is relatively easy to digest. You might have some dinner bites, a little cup of broth-based soup, or something that fits your scheme. Avoid fried foods, large amounts of sugar, dairy products, and very acidic foods as they generally cause bloating and stomach upset following long cycles of fasting.

Reduce intake of alcohol! Reduce it, even if though it is tiny. Alcohol is generally not good for your health, so in intermittent fasting, there is no difference. Alcohol affects your appetite unpredictably on the day you drink, and the day after that. Alcohol and fasting are both highly dehydrating, and as you know, during your fasting, you will need to carry a lot more fluid. You may want to eat starchy food as a result of alcohol; thus, it is very dangerous to your fast. Use common sense and alter your goals to determine how alcohol will affect your tempo. If you're disciplined in alcohol, you'll be able to evaluate the effect of alcohol on your pace and find out how you can adjust to find a way around it while you're just cutting in a heavy drinker. Alcohol is not forbidden, but the amount and frequency in which you decide to take it will affect your fast outcome considerably.

Nothing quickly responds to dramatic changes in the body. Fasting makes adrenaline to be released by the body as it is a gentle type of stress that creates beneficial changes in the body. Adrenaline allows your body to get through resources and energy rapidly. It also raises your heart and metabolism levels, and releases stalled glucose and fat into the blood to provide adequate energy for 'hunting'. If you have trouble sleeping, adrenaline is most likely to cause it. Avoid eating caffeine for a while and have a daily shower to sleep in a quiet, cozy condition to minimize its effects. Use extra energy to complete tasks on your to-do list whenever possible. Adrenaline keeps your metabolic rate high, so your body gets more fat burnt.

Electrolytes are misunderstood by many individuals. They are minerals that perform important functions of the body, such as moving nutrients in and out of cells, supporting constrictions of the muscle and nerve impulses. All electrolytes you should consume regularly are sodium, magnesium, and potassium. Dehydration can cause an imbalance in the electrolyte as its quantity depends on the amount of water in the body. The kidneys excrete more sodium during fasting, which also affects concentrations of potassium and magnesium. You should eat these minerals in your diet to guarantee that your body includes enough minerals. Don't be afraid of salt as it helps in adding sodium to your system in the easiest way. Add salt to tomato slices, broth and salt to your cooking anywhere else as it will make things tasty and help you maintain good levels of sodium. On the other hand, in many food types, magnesium and potassium are discovered differently. Focus on vegetables, fish, milk, nuts, and meat more easily.

Many people consume less magnesium and potassium and that can add to fatigue, weakness, muscle cramps, twitching, and irregular rates of heart. If you notice these signs, the easiest way to restore balance is to take supplements. Too much of each is dangerous; ingredients rich in these minerals are the finest source.

You should eat healthy fat as well. This will make you feel longer full. Fats will not contribute to insulin resistance, as they do not increase insulin levels, unlike carbohydrates. Getting more fats on your tray than carbohydrates will help prevent a low-carbohydrate diet from fighting. There are different types of fat, but only a few of them will add to your health.

Monosaturated fats are found in olives, avocados, and their oils, nuts, and seeds. Eat more monosaturated fats. Saturated fats are found in animal components such as chicken skin or extra fat bacon. Also, dairy products contain high saturated fats. Coconut and palm oils are the only fat-rich plant oils that have been saturated. Saturated fat is misrepresented as a cause of heart disease, but some people get most of their fats and are still okay. Try to be open-minded and don't just stick to one source of fat. Fish and plant products contain omega-3 and omega-6 polyunsaturated fats with two distinct types. More omega-3 and less omega-6 fats should be eaten. For great health, balancing the two is essential. Omega-3 sources of fat are rare, such as cod, mackerel, and crabs. It also has some fruits, but not in its effective form, so it's best to get it from seafood. In almost all processed foods and ingredients, omega-6 fats are not homemade. They are the main type of fat found in seed oils such as soybean and vegetable oil that is cheap, so unless you make a conscious decision to avoid them, you will eat them continuously. The adverse effects of omega-6 are even worse when consumption of omega-3 is low.

You should also know how these fats can be eaten. Cook all in olive oil unless you are looking for a specific taste from cow fat or butter. For baking and roasting products, use olive oil. It is recommended to use olive oil to prepare your dishes, but it is not recommended to fry meat. Eat avocados; they're rich in nutrients and rich in fat. You can eat it the way it is or put it in other food or make potato mash the main point is that it enters our digestive tract. Use avocado oil for cooking if you don't like avocados. Both avocados and olives have large amounts of monosaturated fat. In other simple ways, you can add fats to your diet, such as eating dairy products such as yogurt and cheese, eating whole eggs rather than eating only egg whites, using nut flours such as fruit flour instead of grain flour such as wheat. Take simple coconut milk instead of milk in desserts and smoothies.

Another principle of fasting is not to start fasting under stress. When stressed, your body produces adrenaline and cortisol. It helps the body to overcome stress and get back to normal. The distinction between them is that if the body is under long-term chronic stress, cortisol can remain in high quantities. One of the primary features of cortisol is triggering glucose release into the blood, leading to an increase in insulin concentration. It can help in a momentarily stressful situation, but continually high cortisol levels can retain high blood sugar and glucose, leading to weight gain and eventually, insulin resistance. If due to one cause or another, you are in a stressful point in life, it is advisable not to start a fast. If you want to, it is best to do a short one instead of longer fasts until your stress has disappeared and the body returns to normal conditions.

Types of intermittent fasting

IF regiments are numerous to the point that you can choose from any that you like. Always make sure to select a regiment that will fit in your schedule so that it is possible to maintain it.

There are several short schedules for fasting, including:

The 12-hour fast

That's what the normal living routine is called as you eat three meals a day and fast at night as you sleep. The generally small breakfast would break the fast. It is called the traditional method. Any regiment can help you lose weight only if you follow it properly.

The higher the levels of insulin are as a result of more people adding regular eating and snacking. This can cause resistance to insulin and ultimately, obesity. This technique of fasting sets aside twelve hours in which the body has low levels of insulin, reducing the likelihood of insulin resistance. It can't help you lose excess fat, but it can help prevent obesity.

The 16-hour fast

This fasting for 16 hours, followed by an 8-hour window where you can eat what you like. Luckily you can sleep through most of it, so it's not difficult to keep doing it. Because it requires only small changes like just skipping your lunch, it has an enormous advantage over others, such as the 12 hours fast.

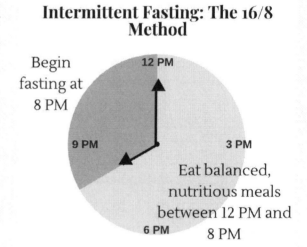

Intermittent Fasting: The 16/8 Method

The 20-hour fast

It's called the' warrior diet.' It includes fasting all day long and eating a lot of calories at night. It's meant to keep you from having breakfast, lunch and other meals for most of the day, so you're getting all your nutrients from dinner. It is a division scheme of 20:4 with four hours of food followed by twenty hours of fasting. It's one of the easiest to do as you're allowed to eat a huge meal of calorific value, so you're going to feel fuller for longer. Start your daytime calories and have a big evening dinner to relax in this diet. You're going to gradually reduce what you're eating during the day and eventually leave dinner as your only dinner.

Eating foods such as healthy fruits and vegetables and staying hydrated with water is permitted during the fasting period. In order to maintain your calorie concentrations, your dinner should involve huge amounts of healthy fats and protein. It's a challenging task to start with this fasting method, but always make sure that you don't eat any big meal outside the fast as you end it.

Your four hours eating time is not specifically set for dinner; it can even be breakfast or lunch; it depends on what you decide. Whatever you make up your mind, the laws remain the same. While you can decide when to set the time to eat, it is better to put it earlier. This is because your body is in a better position to handle fat and sugar in the morning rather than in the evening as it is compelled to start digestion at that moment. Your morning systems will be active, so your body will not be bothered by digestion.

These short regiments are called time-limited eating regiments. They are widely used by celebrities, bodybuilders, and millennials. Even

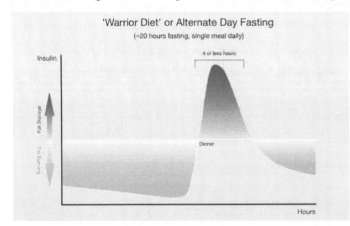

Buddha advised people not to ingest anything after lunch and to eat the next morning to his disciples as it would give them a sense of well-being and tranquility. Researchers have conducted extensive studies on these schemes and have seen a huge distinction between those who adopt this scheme and those who consume whenever they feel it. The same food you can eat, but what matters is the time. Upon reaching your goal, you can go back with the fasting regiment to your regular feeding system or continue with it.

This method of fasting gives you numerous advantages. It can work with your circadian rhythm, the inner clock of the body. It responds to dark and light, impacting your hunger, sleepiness, and renaissance physiological indicators. Eating during the day works better with the circadian rhythms than eating at night because paleolithic people consumed most of their food during the day. Time-limited eating also helps eradicate issues such as late-night snacking, which can affect your insulin concentration seriously. That's because there's no eating at all once your eating window is closed, so you're going to conquer such poor procedures.

The longer you do these fasting regiments, the more you will be able to maintain a fast. You will come to find out that you will not always feel hungry. The excitement of benefits will make you increase your period of fasting by a couple of hours. Unknowingly, therefore, you are plunging into longer stages of fasting. You can adhere to your regiment religiously, but eating an extra hour will not ruin your fasting or fat burning.

The easiest way to track your feeding is to do it once a day because it doesn't require a lot of thought. It's just eating at that moment every day on one dinner, so you can use your mental energy on more significant stuff. Unfortunately, it can cause a plateau of weight loss, where you are not losing or gaining weight. That's because you're going to consume the same amount of calories every day and significantly less on a standard working day than you would eat. That's the best way to maintain your weight. You will have to change your fasting regiment to lose fat after a while. Timing your meals and fasting windows will lead to optimal loss of fat instead of random fasting. Choose one that can be maintained and modified if necessary.

There are longer fasting regiments, these include:

The 24-hour fast

It's a scheme of eating breakfast, lunch or dinner in a day and then eating the next day at the same time. If you decide to eat lunch then it only involves skipping breakfast and dinner, so nothing is disrupted in your life. It saves time and money because you're not going to eat as much and piling up dishes will not be a worry of yours. Knowing that you are fasting will be a task for people unless they are very interested in eating methods. By eating unprocessed natural foods, you should have enough vitamins, minerals, and oxygen to avoid nutrient deficiencies. You can do this weekly, but twice or three times a week is the best suggestion.

During such long fasts, you should not knowingly avoid eating calories. What you are taking should be high in fat, low in carbohydrates, and unprocessed; there's nothing you shouldn't eat. You should consume until you are adequately fed as the duration of fasting lets you burn a bunch of fat, and it will be difficult over time to try to cut more purposefully.

The 36-hour fast

You maintain fasting for one and a half days without eating. For instance, if you eat lunch today, you consume no meal until the breakfast of the day after the next day. This type of fast should be done about three times a week for people with type 2 diabetes. After the person reaches the desired weight and all diabetes medications are successfully removed, he or she can reduce the number of days of fasting to a level that will make it easier for the person to do while maintaining their gains. The longer the person was diagnosed with diabetes, the longer the plan is going to last. During this period it is advisable to check the level of sugar in the blood.

The 42-hour fast

This is adding six hours to the 36 hour fast resulting in a fast of forty-two hours that can be carried out about two times a week.

The 5:2 fast

This technique is conducted to prevent you from totally abstaining from meals, but to have cycles of calorie consumption. These calories are reduced to a rate that leads to many hormonal advantages of fasting. Five days of ordinary feeding with two days of fasting. With some protein and oil-based sauce or green vegetables and half an avocado, you can eat some vegetable salad during these fasting days furthermore, do not eat any dinner. These days of fasting can be placed randomly or following each other in a week at specific times. This method is designed to make fast accessible to more people, as many find it difficult to avoid eating altogether. There's no clear time to follow; as soon as you want, you can start it.

The alternate-day fast

This may seem similar to the 5:2 fasting regimen, but it is not. It's fasting every other day. This technique can be followed until you lose as much weight as you want, then you can reduce days of fasting. It allows weight loss to be maintained.

It is possible to move to different fasting regiments as your schedule can change. Intermittent fasting is not about a time-limiting eating window, it is a flexible approach, so you can move your eating and fasting time to suit you, but don't keep changing them all the time; this reduces the effect of fasting on your body. You can even combine some fasting regiments like the 5:2 technique and the 24-hour fasting by having lunch before your fasting day at a certain moment and adding only lunch at the fasting lunch and doing the same for the next fasting day. With this, for twenty-four hours, you could not eat any calories and set your days of fasting as in the 5:2 method of fasting. Choose the fasting day technique that works well with you and can synchronize with your life.

A schedule allows you to create a routine after frequent fasting that makes it easier to integrate into your life. You can plan, but there's no problem if you can't. Even if you can't plan to fast, you should be open-minded and fasting to opportunities. You can fast every month or every year. Frankly, you won't lose weight on losing annual fasts.

Advantages and disadvantages of intermittent fasting

Intermittent fasting certainly has many advantages to be discussed for the body, and some downsides later. Luckily, the benefits of intermittent fasting overshadow downsides.

Intermittent advantages of fasting include:

1. A home-cooked dinner has many health benefits, but you do not always have the time or willingness to eat. Fortunately, intermittent fasting is favorable. Many things in this days occupy most people's time, so they cannot find the time to cook when they are not tired. Fasting saves time because you don't always have to cook, shop for food, or prepare ingredients. Usually, it makes life a lot easier. All it involves is doing the easiest thing.

2. It reduces insulin levels and insulin resistance most simply and easily. It is has a very strong effect. It has more impact than the ketogenic diet. It can help break through rigid weight-loss plateaus. There is no limit, so you can fast as much as you want to. You can enhance the frequency and length of your fasting to reduce your time to achieve your goal. Meanwhile, there are

limitations to medicines. It becomes poisonous if you carry more than the maximum dose and can even lead to death. Even low carbohydrate or fat diets have limits; you can't do much more to burn fat once you've got zero carbs and fats in your diet. Some diets can also work with some people whilst fasting is for everyone.

3. It is cost-effective. Organic food like grass-fed beef and wise over-processed food ingredient greens tower. These organic foods are costly, unfortunately, so buying them every day will only drain your pockets. In fact, they are ten times more costly than processed food. Clearly, the best cost-effective alternative is to feed on processed products. While a diet is efficient as soon as it is not inexpensive, it will not damage you. Fast here is a winning situation as you will not spend a lot of money. Yes, it's completely safe. You don't have to buy meals, so it will save you money. Fasting does not require you to buy expensive meals or supplements, or any medication that makes it the most cost-effective for all.

4. It improves your physiology Fasting intermittent decreases the number of calories you carry in a day considerably. During the fasting period, it is almost impossible to eat the daily suggested quantity of calories. This helps to modify the body and burn fat. It will also help you eat fat even if you bring the standard calorie quantity as your body uses fat for energy instead of carbohydrates.

5. If you decide to start dieting you are going to have to forfeit some ingredients indefinitely like chocolate or ice cream, which is great for burning fat but not for you as an individual, these may never be tasted again. These cutbacks may seem minor, but it is a long sentence to cut them off indefinitely. If you indulge in such

pleasures, fasting saves the day. This doesn't mean you're taking junk food every day as doing so will damage yourself; rather, it means loving these products in moderation. Fasting is very suitable for specific circumstances; if you can help them with abstinence, you can indulge yourself. It's about the best balance between good and unhealthy ingredients. You should also keep the time you eat and the time you don't getting the maximum benefit for you.

6. Intermittent fasting can take place at any time; this is very flexible. It is not as challenging as some diets that massively interfere with your lives unnecessarily. There is no specific duration to do intermittent fasting. They can be mixed up to fit for your schedule. There's no point in you being packed into a regiment that isn't easy to maintain. Fasting intermittent adjusts the unpredictability of life. It can be done anywhere in any part of the globe because it's not something you need to do, it's just nutrition limiting, so it's much simpler and more practical than many diets. Even if for a while you have to stop fasting, it's okay. Fasting can start in minutes again.

7. Intermittent fasting requires no hard scheduling, eating, and drinking water is easy. This makes it easier to follow than many other diets and more efficient.

8. It encourages the secretion of growth hormone. Intermittent fasting increases the secretion of growth hormone. It has been discovered more in children than in adolescents, but it never helps much less. Growth hormone reduces body fat, increasing the development of bone and muscle. To deliver glucose into the bloodstream, it breaks down glycogen. This helps to promote muscle loss-free fat burning. With enough sleep and practice, the growth hormone also increases.

9. It enhances your reception and control of hormones. Intermittent fasting leaves small concentrations of insulin in the body, making it susceptible to small increases. If you take too much sugar, your effects will eventually become numb as your concentrations of insulin will constantly increase. Your reception of insulin is very important because insulin is associated with diabetes-like diseases. Developments in insulin resistance will prevent the body from gaining fat deposits.

10. It helps to control the mental procedures of your body. You are used to fulfilling the wishes of your body because you eat three meals a day. Intermittent Fasting frees you from being controlled by your body. Your body will first try to fight back, but the uprising will eventually subside as it adapts. This will release your mind, allowing you to focus on more important things and repairing your body. It also helps to improve the health of the brain. It improves the output of BDNF, a protein that protects brain cells from degenerative neurological disorders. You're going to feel great overall brain health.

11. It can synchronize with any diet regardless of what you eat and what you don't eat, you can still swift. No foods are forbidden.

12. It helps prevent heart disease. Regulating blood sugar and reducing fat are both things accomplished through intermittent fasting that enhance heart health.

With intermittent fasting, there are comparatively few dangers if you are well-nourished for starters, but there still are. They include the following:

1. If you have a medical condition, this type of fasting can have a negative effect on your health. Throughout the day, for example, people who are hypoglycemic need glucose, so intermittent fasting cannot be a benefit.

2. Having low energy. While after a while, hunger will go away, you still can predict what can happen in your life. You may find yourself engaged in an exercise that will make you hungry and unproductive until the hunger is gone. You may already eat a bunch of meals in a day and stop by fasting suddenly; this may contribute to some side effects. They include headaches, lack of energy, constipation, and poor concentration. It can also lower the drive for activity.

3. Intermittent fasting reduces the body's dependence on energy on carbohydrates, making it more dependent on fats. This increases the stored breakdown of fat. As a reaction to the decrease of severe body energy intake, the body can create physiological adaptations. Simply put, this means that after severe food restriction, you may not be able to keep your new weight or gain even more weight.

4. It can cause some digestive complications. Taking a large dinner creates digestion problems very quickly. Individuals tend to have larger snacks in the intermittent fasting eating window, leading to a longer digestive moment. This makes your digestive tract more stressful, leading to indigestion and bloating. This has a greater impact on sensitive guts.

5. It can result in social eating disruption. Eating is an extremely social activity. Special occasions, celebrations, milestone finishing, and other important occasions all involve sharing food with people close to you. Intermittent fasting may interfere with your social occasions as you change patterns and may not match the regular pattern. Because of the short window, in events where everyone is merrily eating and drinking, you may have to eat or be the odd out. Among many others, you will skip many eating activities such as dinner conferences, family dinners, and late-night romantic meals.

6. If the fasting regiment is done in a way that largely restricts protein and sugars, it is highly likely to cause fertility problems in women, cause anomalies in electrolytes, may be caused by nutrient deficiencies. Intermittent fasting involves issues related to menstruation, early menopause, and fertility. Research shows that it can decrease the ovarian size in addition to decreasing body size, thus affecting reproduction.

7. Food restriction is a very good practice done during intermittent fasting. However, people are using the eating window to eat a lot which is not right. They eventually take more calories than they need to undo the calorie deficit created by the period of fasting. It's very attractive but strongly warned against it.

Keto and
Intermittent Fasting

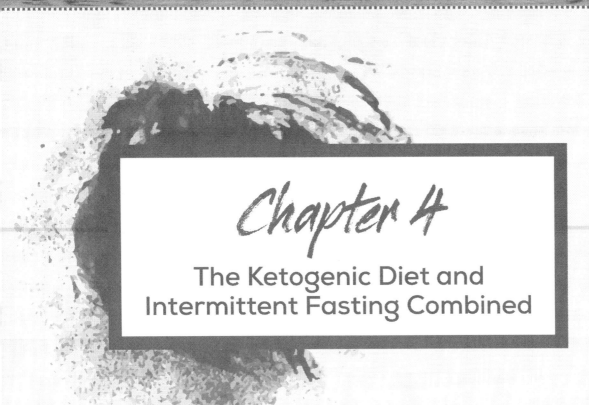

Chapter 4
The Ketogenic Diet and Intermittent Fasting Combined

Intermittent fasting can help you achieve ketosis more rapidly than after practicing a ketogenic diet alone. This is feasible as the body gets its energy from fats instead of carbohydrates when you practice intermittent fasting as well as the ketogenic diet. So if you discover it difficult to enter a ketosis state, it can greatly assist you.

Food quality is more important than the amount here. Ideal products include grass-fed meat, pasture-grown hens' eggs, grass-fed butter and cheese, fruit, organic creams, and vegetables. They are ideal, but eating standard foods won't prevent ketosis from occurring. Do what you can to consume food of high quality.

In the ketogenic diet, you should consume lots of fat as they are the main source of energy, which doesn't imply you can eat fat without limit. There are some good fats for you and others that aren't. A lot of saturated fats from poultry, eggs, meat, coconut, and butter must be eaten: polyunsaturated fats such as tuna and salmon; and monounsaturated fats such as nuts, nut butter, avocado, and olive oil. It is important to avoid highly produced polyunsaturated fats such as vegetable oil and soybean oil.

It is possible to obtain protein from many sources of fat, such as meat and eggs. You can also consume protein and fat in bacon and sausages. In order to maintain you in ketosis, you should consume within the suggested quantity of protein as your body transforms surplus protein into glucose.

Since fruits contain sugar, however natural they may be, they will boost your blood glucose and pull you out from ketosis state. Fruits are not completely prohibited; it relies on your consumption amount. It is best to produce fruits elevated in fiber and low in carbohydrates. On the other side, vegetables are essential because they supply minerals and vitamins without adding a lot of calories. They are helping to keep you safe. Some vegetables are full of carbohydrates, so the ketogenic diet is not permitted for all vegetables. Eat vegetables such as spinach, broccoli and green beans, asparagus, cucumbers, and mushrooms, leafy or pale green. Keep away from starchy vegetables such as white potatoes, yams, maize, and sweet potatoes.

Full-fat dairy is common in a ketogenic diet. Use heavy cream, sour cream, hard cheese, butter, and cottage cheese to help you satisfy your fat requirements. Avoid dairy products that are low-fat and flavored as they are full of sugar.

Water is the finest drink you can consume. You should always try to drink in ounces about half of your body weight. Unsweetened tea and coffee are permitted. Keep away from sodas, flavored water, sweetened lemon aid; basically any sweet beverage from fruit juice you can fuse it with fresh herbs to add thrill to simple water.

Grain and sugar consumption should be prevented in all types. Grains are like rice, rye, wheat, sorghum, barley, and any of its products. This means no pasta, no bread, and no crackers. It is not permitted to use honey, brown and white sugar, maple syrup, and anything else that includes sugar. Make sure there is no sugar in what you consume.

The combination of the two can lead to fat melting quicker than each on its own. During intermittent fasting, your body utilizes stubborn fat as it encourages metabolism that results in heat manufacture. This helps preserve muscle mass during weight loss and increases energy levels for keto dieters who want to lose weight and improve their athletic prowess. Combining the scheme of intermittent fasting and the ketogenic diet can lead to more body fat melting than individuals who follows IF but still consume junk food.

It can also increase your body structure as intermittent fasting improves human growth hormone output but at very large proportion. This hormone performs an enormous part in constructing muscles. The human growth hormone helps an individual reducing body fat concentrations and boost lean body and bone mass, according to studies conducted. Working out in a fasted state can result in metabolic adjustments in your muscle cells arising in energy fat burning. The human growth hormone also enables you to recover from injury or even difficult exercise at a quicker pace. It also decreases skin swelling. It enhances the strength of your skin to wrinkles and sagging.

The mixture of the two can even affect the aging process in a beneficial way. They cause the process of stem cells to rise. These are like construction blocks for the body as they can be transformed into any cell the body requires, as well as replacing ancient or harmed cells that keep you younger internally for longer. These stem cells can do wonders to old wounds, chronic pain, and much more. This can enhance your life expectaction as your general health is enhanced by balancing blood glucose, reducing swelling, and improving the free radical defense.

It can boost autophagy. This is simply cell cleaning measures. When it starts, your cells migrate through your inner components and remove any harmed or old cells and replace them with fresh ones. It's like an organ upgrade. It decreases inflammation and improves organ life.

There are no cravings, tiredness, and mood changes when exercising the ketogenic diet and intermittent fasting. This is accomplished through constantly small concentrations of blood sugar. This is because your blood sugar concentrations are not increased by fat. You will be prepared to keep small concentrations of blood sugar that can significantly assist individuals with Type 2 diabetes, even get off their drugs.

The liver transforms fat into packets of energy called ketones that are taken into the blood to offer your cells energy. These ketones destroy the ghrelin, the primary hunger hormone. High concentrations of ghrelin leave you famished while ketones decrease hormone concentrations even if your digestive tract does not contain any meals. This means you can stay without eating for a longer period of time and you won't get hungry. Undoubtedly, the ketogenic diet makes fasting much easier for you to do.

Some individuals follow the ketogenic diet integrated with intermittent fasting. This is by observing the ketogenic nutritional laws while also pursuing the trend of intermittent fasting eating. This can have many advantages, including high-fat burning levels, as both are important in using fats for energy over carbohydrates, providing you energy, reducing cholesterol in your body, controlling your blood sugar that can assist manage type 2 diabetes, helping to cope with hunger, and reducing skin inflammation.

For most individuals, combining the two is comfortable and can significantly speed up the fat burning process, making you accomplish your objectives quicker. However, one or the other can be done alone as they have many comparable advantages. Choosing an intermittent fasting unit that fits you is also essential and always makes sure you consume enough of the macro ingredients. Depending on what was in the meals, the functions can be comparatively fine for both. The job performed will be ideal when you mix both of them and will make weight loss much easier for you to do as both operate in distinct aspects but complement each other superbly.

Chapter 5
Weight Loss and Exercise

We all know that exercise is good for you and that it can help you lose weight, but we don't necessarily do it. Many individuals are giving the excuse that they don't want to be huge and bulky or that they don't have enough time, the truth is a lot of people don't like to exercise and get bored. You will learn a simple workout that you can do in no time; thus, you won't have any excuse to practice anymore. Exercise keeps you healthy, glad, and enables you to sleep much easier.

Contrary to the common faith, working out on days of fasting can effectively lead to a greater level of muscle building and fat burning than working out on normal days. Noradrenaline concentrations are greater when fasting, enabling you to practice harder while increasing the concentrations of human growth hormone assist in boosting muscle mass. Misinformed and uninformed individuals indicate that fasting lowers muscle mass, which is not a fact.

If you want to burn fat by following any diet or regiment, one fact that remains constant is that you have to take fewer calories than you burn. You need to generate a calorie deficit of that quantity to lose a certain quantity. You can't locate a fat-burning post or book and forget the term ' calories', so what are they? These are food's energy. Every action in your body is powered by calories, so your body needs them constantly.

Calories are obtained from carbohydrates, fats, and proteins and are your body's primary source of energy. They are either used as physical energy or deposited as body fat regardless of where they came from. Stored calories will remain as fat in your body unless they are used up by reducing the intake of calories so that your body can use up the reserves or by burning more calories than you take in by physical exercise. It's great for you to exercise and it makes you feel good.

How do you calculate the calories you eat, the calories you need to burn, and the calories you burned during your workout? Check the nutritional content of the food supplied on the back or side of the box to calculate the number of calories in the food you bought from the store. There are distinct quantities of calories per unit in each macronutrient. Twenty grams of protein includes four calories, 35 grams of carbohydrate includes four calories, and 15 grams of fat includes nine calories. Calculate the food's calorific value by multiplying the caloric equal of each macronutrient. These nutrients are always calculated in grams. To discover the complete calories of the meals, add the calories provided off by each macronutrient. When calculating the number of calories like this, you will not only find out the calorific value, but you will also be able to incorporate it into a balanced diet. The serving size and the number of servings contained must be taken into account. Nearly all of them indicate only one serving's calorific amount, the number of servings can actually alter the calorie count. Always compare the number of nutrients you are taking with the recommended values, so you don't eat too much or too little. Online calculators and guide books can also be used to help you do this.

You should first know your basal metabolic rate to know how many calories you burn during the workout session. This is the amount of energy that your body uses to work. There is no constant number because everything depends on several factors. Age is one of the determining factors for your BMR. The older you are, the lower your BMR, the more exercise you will need. A muscular person is more likely to burn more fat than a fat person. The ambient temperature also serves apart as the greater your BMR will be. The hotter it is, the higher your BMR this is because you are warmed up by the setting, so more calories are invested in losing weight. Work out duration is also a major factor, the better, the longer, but don't overdo it. The fitter you are, the fewer calories you are going to consume as your body is already used to it. Your diet has a direct effect on your metabolism. If you don't consume enough, drink too much, or exercise any other poor dietary habits, your metabolism will be impacted, thus decreasing the number of calories you burn. Lack of sufficient sleep can cause you to consume more calories as you become more exhausted, and practice is more probable, but it can also impact your metabolism. Oxygen helps to offer energy to your body to continue to work. You will consume more calories if you breathe more strongly during workouts.

Some common methods are available to approximate the number of calories you burn in a day. Everyone has their strengths and weaknesses, so it's best to use them all and use the mean as the estimate for the best results. The first is by using exercise devices such as the Fit bit to monitor your regular motions and assess calories consumed during the period they are held. While it has been discovered that the amount of calories burned is not entirely precise, they are very handy and simple to use. Metabolic screening is another technique. The machinery needed for this technique in laboratories and clinics that can be accessed affordably from there as they are very expensive. These examinations can assist you in changing what you eat and your exercise regiment, but some individuals do not think the price of this technique is worth it. Always try to ensure that you are tested by a skilled technician so you can get the most accurate results. The last but mostly used is online calculators. These calculators are trying to offer your weekly spending an estimated value. The amount they offer is very general, but they can be used as your weight loss guideline. Calculating the mean of all these techniques will offer you a near assessment of how many calories you consume in a day.

Yes, exercising on an empty stomach is okay and secure. A generally healthy adult can generally practice on an empty stomach without having any negative reactions. Working out without eating will result in you burning more body fat. You are more probable to have more energy, when you're in a fasted state, to do your workout routine.

However, if you have experienced fainting, feeling dizzy or weak after practice during a fasted state, do not continue doing it. Always listen to your body; without even knowing it, you might destroy it. By organizing an exercise timetable that operates well with your fasting timetable as you can organize your time table any direction you like, you can work out around this. Exercising while fasting can speed up the weight loss process.

There is a fat-burning myth that you have to eat fat to lose body fat when you exercise. It may seem embarrassing but by reading on you will discover that this is not true. People also believe that carrying out an aerobic workout with peak paces encourages fat loss, and that low intensity exercising the quantity of fat used is low, leading to the equation that the more the intensity of the exercise the highest the quantity of fat used.

The impacts of various intensities of aerobic exercise have been compared, and the prevalent finding is that the total fat loss is equivalent regardless of the strength at which the practice was performed, provided the caloric consumption is the same. This implies that the quantity of calories used during practice is more essential than the energy used. The body decreases fat as soon as it burns more calories than it eats. Exercise intensity and length are inversely proportional. The higher the intensity of activity requires, the lower the workout length. For a lengthy period you can attempt a low-intensity exercise or high-intensity exercise for a brief period, see what fits your body best.

If you want a strong heart and lungs, you should look after your body. Strength training is essential. There's no doubt that exercising makes you feel nice, and it also assists you to burn calories while you're sleeping. If you enhance your muscle amount, your sensitivity to insulin will also increase. In order to assist you to boost your muscle mass, you should develop a fitness exercise scheme to reduce your weight and improve muscle mass.

During aerobic exercise, the calorie expenditure is on average five calories/minute during a low-intensity workout and around ten calories/minute during a high-intensity workout. Two exercise days, even if you burn more calories, does not equal the fat-burning of losing calories across several days. You should exercise like three times/week, but the division between weights, interval training, and weights depends on your goals.

If you do exercise, but you do not change your diet, your weight loss process will be very slow. It is not easy as it will reach a point that the amount of fat you will burn will be directly proportional to the amount and time you spend exercising. About nine calories/minute are used during weight training. On top of burning calories through exercise, there are also more calories lost after the exercise, which is called excess post-exercise oxygen consumption. It is as a result of an increase in adrenalin and noradrenalin on top of other factors that make your system burn calories even after exercise from the fat stores. The magnitude of the post-exercise calorie loss is dependent on the intensity and duration in which the exercise was carried out. Not many people can be able to sustain energy to the point that they generate a large EPOC.

Dieting without exercise is a common approach people undertake. The problem with it is that it leads to a loss in lean body mass and reduced metabolic rate. To make up for the calorie restriction, the system lowers the metabolic rate. As a result, your body can enter starvation mode; thus you will not lose any more weight. When food intake is returned, the lowered metabolism results in regain of the fat that was lost. It is not an effective long term plan. If you eat too little and exercise more, you may enter into starvation mode, which can stop fat loss completely. Achieving the balance between exercise and dietary alterations to enhance weight loss while preventing muscle loss is the ultimate goal. Getting more muscular will raise your metabolic rate.

High-interval intensity training, HIIT, is an exercise method that works incredibly to promote weight loss and results in greater weight loss than lower intensity continuous workout. You simply switch between periods of high-intensity activity and periods of low-intensity activity. The practice can suit your timetable, however tight your schedule is. It allows you in a short time to get the advantages of lengthy workout sessions. There are different kinds of intermittent excercising you can attempt. If you like cycling, you could: warm-up with soft cycling, start pedaling after a minute as you do and boost the strength, after 15 seconds your bodies get tired, if you can proceed at the same speed then the strength you set is not big enough, you will discover your ideal tough resistance after practicing severely, after fast-cycling reduces the strength. By walking, swimming and any other workout that can be performed quickly, you can also do HIIT without a bicycle.

There are several small changes you are making to increase the amount of activity you are doing in your life. You should use a basket instead of using a trolley when shopping to get some resistance training as you do your shopping. Instead of escalators, use stairs to get some leg training. Drink plenty of water not just to get hydrated, but so you can get up and go to the bathroom once in a while. When going to a near location, it is best for you to just walk there instead of driving or using the bus. When you get any opportunity use a bicycle and cycle around, you don't necessarily require a destination it's easier than running and has many advantages. Stand up when you're on the bus to use more calories. If you're taking a bus to get to your job, or drive, get off the bus before your stop or park away from your ordinary location so you can walk the remainder of the distance. The more, the merrier, arrange lunchtime walking groups to get other people's support. Be spontaneous, begin dance classes, this will make you progress more, feel good and rejuvenated, and they're interesting as well.

Standing is one of the simplest forms of exercising. Yes, it's that easy, it's just stand up. After every thirty minutes if you have been sitting, just stand. It's terrible for your health to sit continually for lengthy stretches of time. The simplest way to do is to set the alarm after every half hour on your mobile to remind you to wake up and walk a little. Even if you're a strong TV watcher, you can stand during commercial breaks or after the episode of the series you are watching ends.

Another easy activity you can do is walking. It's very inexpensive and secure, and in the morning it is best accomplished. If you have no leg impairment, it's so simple that you can't get it wrong. Morning walks can assist enhance your metabolism, and it also enables you to get early morning sun vitamin D. Morning light from the sun helps reset your inner clock, leading in better night sleep. You can bring a partner or a member of your community to make it more enjoyable and simpler to do.

When you practice, your body requires an enhanced quantity of energy. It will use glucose for energy first, and then use glycogen once it is exhausted. Increased demand for energy-requiring practice leads to quicker depletion of glycogen; otherwise, enough glycogen is collected in the liver for 24-hour use. This quantity depends on the length and intensity of the workout. Once glycogen is exhausted, the body starts to burn fat. Your capacity to burn fat is governed by your sympathetic nervous system that is triggered through practice and fasting. The mixture of the two maximizes the procedures of physiology that break down energy fat. Unlike storage of glycogen, there is no limit to fat storage, so you can never run out. Your muscles will get used to using whatever energy source you offer them, body fat in this situation, with continuous practice.

Fasted practice can also assist glucose concentrations and growth hormone concentrations in addition to burning fat. Fasted exercise provides your body a break from insulin release and also helps you complete any insulin your body might have. Your body's healthy insulin reaction can facilitate fat loss and also improve blood flow to muscles, making muscle building simpler. As a result of practice, enhanced growth hormone output helps burn fat and boost muscle tissue and increases bone health. Regular practice is an essential component of remaining healthy, so it is essential to plan properly for a periodic workout to make your environment enjoyable. Always listen to the particular requirements of your body when choosing this stuff.

It's a common conviction that you should eat tiny snacks frequently to maintain your metabolism healthy. That's why you may discover individuals saying that six tiny dishes are better than three big dishes distributed throughout the day. In fact, when you are in a fasted state, your basal metabolic rate rises considerably. This is because your blood norepinephrine and neurotransmitter will reduce when you fast. This stimulates your metabolism and indicates that surplus body fats breakdown.

30 minute HIIT Workout

1. Do 2 sets of squats each with 6-8 reps and rest for 90 seconds between each set

2. Do 1 set of calf raises each with 8-10 reps and rest for 60 seconds between each set

3. Do 1 set of leg curls each with 8-10 reps and rest for 60 seconds between each set

4. Do 2 sets of bench presses each with 6-8 reps and rest for 90 seconds between each set

5. Do 2 sets of the row each with 6-8 reps and rest for 90 seconds between each set

6. Do 1 set of shoulder press each with 8-10 reps and rest for 60 seconds between each set

7. Do 1 set of pull-down to front each with 8-10 reps and rest for 90 seconds between each set

8. Do 2 sets of crunches each with 12-15 reps and rest for 60 seconds between each set

9. Do 1 set of triceps pushdown each with 12-15 reps and rest for 60 seconds between each set

10. Do 1 set of arm curls each with 12-15 reps and rest for 60 seconds between each set

11. Do 1 set of back extension each with 8-12 reps and rest for 60 seconds between each set

Always remember to do 1-2 warm-up
sets before these exercises.

Keto and
Intermittent Fasting

Chapter 6
How to Enhance Weight Loss for You

By now, you know so much about rapid weight loss. The information is effective for the general public, but the main person this information is intended for is you as an individual. There are many ways for you to make this weight loss more effective for you.

You should keep a diary. In this diary, you should record what you're feeling while following the ketogenic diet together with intermittent fasting. This includes all the highs and lows. You should also keep track of the food you're consuming; this includes the time, amount, and even the calorific value so that you have detailed information that you can refer to when you require to. You can also change the food you are eating as long as the food you decide to eat falls in the ketogenic diet restrictions.

You should try to have fun during the weight loss burning as it is improving your life quality and duration. Do not be shaken by small setbacks such as eating outside of the rules of the diet or the fasting the regiment since we all fall sometimes as no one is perfect, the only time you fail is when you decide to stop following them completely.

The main issue that occurs in the first few weeks of following these regiments is hunger. It will end with time, but the hunger period poses a huge challenge for many people. In order to be able to overcome hunger pangs, there are several things you can do. They are discussed below.

Make it a point for you to understand why you want some meals; is it because of the boredom of real thirst and hunger? Are you just exhausted or agitated and in search of food for satisfaction? Try your best to distract yourself so that during your period of fasting so that you don't wind up eating. You should always offer hope to yourself that you will find it through the time of yearning. It is going to happen, but it will eventually go away.

Give your body time to adjust to the new diet and fasting regiment. No living organism readily accepts the transition from one condition to another; this is why evolution takes place in millions of years, your body will have to get used to the fresh lifestyle you've begun and can respond to meals differently. Headaches, hunger, and even body failure are among the probable discomforts. You may be proceeding slowly, but in the correct direction, it is said that it is to have direction than velocity. Don't submit to your urges.

At moments we're all compelled by different foodstuffs that may have no real nutritive value, but we still desire them. Removing from your place of living or around your work desk, these products will create it much simpler not to be encouraged to consume them.

At first, if you find the following of recipes to be too hard, you can replace them with shakes as you get used to them.

Organize your timetable. You can choose a window to eat and discover that at that time you don't have time to eat. Don't set your eating window at a moment when you know it's going to be difficult to go without food as if you're eating when you're bored and don't set your eating time during the time the day is boring. If at a certain point you have dinner with your relatives, then at that time should be placed in your eating window. When choosing on your feeding window, make wise decisions. It's always best to create a schedule that will make following it as simple as feasible.

Be the pillar of your own journey. There's always this voice in your head when you're hungry that provides you many explanations why breaking your diet is the best option. When we are fragile, it gets even the best of us. Not listening to that voice is essential to you. Even if only once you break the fast or diet, you will eventually do it over and over again. Staying powerful is best for maximum weight loss. If you give in, then don't use it as an excuse to stop fasting entirely, continue trying because when you stop attempting, you will not lose weight or achieve your goals.

Set definite objectives you'd like to accomplish. What are you aiming to achieve with this regiment of fasting? With increasing difficulty, having generic reasons to continue with the diet, and fasting regiment like wanting to lose some weight will not motivate you. Your reasons should hold more meaning to you like wanting to lose weight so as to prevent you from having another stroke or whatever that is in your life. If you don't have a definite reason to do a fast or diet, you're more inclined to stop following it than someone with particular objectives. In the near future, and also, in the long run, you should know what you want to achieve. What scale mark do you want to be below in three months? What do you want your blood pressure to be in six months? In twelve months, do you want to wear those clothes you have in your closet but cannot fit you because of your size?? All these and more are the questions that you should ask yourself. Even after knowing what you want in those periods of time, you should also ask yourself why you want those things and if it is achieved, the effect of the goal on your life. This enables you to see items more important to you. If you are eager to consume that additional piece of cake, remember how your life will be altered in the end if you accomplish your objectives.

Besides individual assistance, you can also receive additional assistance from other people. Make it a point to have individuals around you who are on the same journey to weight loss as you. It's going to get tough and quitting seems like the only choice, but if you have other individuals to support you, it's going to aid in you in persevering. The stronger you can sustain each other, the more of will achieve your goals.

Be patient. You might think of IF and the keto diet as the magic bullets you can use to burn all your fat instantly, but it's not possible. It takes time for all nice stuff like fat burning and hormone changes to take place, so try to be patient. Only if you stay constant through the regiments will you ultimately see excellent outcomes.

Remain hydrated. The body can sometimes interpret dehydration as hunger. Sometimes you may believe you're famished while you're only thirsty in the real sense. Drink plenty of water, black coffee, sparkling water, black tea, or other zero-calorie drinks.

Sleep is one of the main aspects of weight loss that can assist you in achieving rapid weight loss that many overlook. Many information sources don't give enough weight to the significance of sleep. Proper sleep can increase a big proportion of your general fasting outcomes. Our organs repair damage when you sleep, burn fat, and switch cells.

The quality, as well as the amount, matter a lot in sleep.

There are different methods to improve your sleep quality. First, get more light from the sun. Your "body clock" don't comprehend time the same way you do; it understands time through the use of light signals. It is strongly influenced by sunlight. Morning sunlight is signaling your glands and organs to wake up to generate hormones that should be used during the day. If you get a little daytime sunlight, and on top of that, a lot of nighttime artificial light, our circadian clock will be decalibrated. This malfunction can create hormones in your body that can stop you from sleeping. If you don't get enough quality sleep, substances like glucose and the manufacturing of substances like HGH can boost not allowing fat to be burned at night.

It is best for you to make an effort to avoid all screens and light before you go to sleep. If you fall asleep watching television or while using your mobile, you might not be getting all the beneficial effects of the fast as we sleep. Not only sunlight affects your body clock, but also artificial light. These displays generate mostly blue light, which causes our body to generate hormones designed to make you stay awake and active. It'll be difficult to fall asleep. Always strive to make it a routine to avoid these devices before sleeping as it will benefit you more than you think. Sleeping in darkness is best for your body clock and hormones. Black out your windows or put up heavy-duty curtains when there are annoying street lights, and other sources of light outside you can't regulate.

There's a certain amount of time in the evening that while you sleep your body generates the finest amount of hormones needed to lose weight. It's best to get into bed as soon as night falls as often as feasible. General health, loss of weight, and strengthening of muscles are just some of the many advantages of enhancing your sleep. It can have a stronger effect on your weight loss journey than even increasing your workout time.

Success stories

As these weight loss regiments are based on facts, here are some true success stories to back them up.

One of the people who were brave enough to share their story is called Jane. Within one year she changed her life while following the keto diet and IF combo. This what she had to say:

I never thought that I would share my story, but after a lot of encouragement, here goes.

In October 2016, I had been on a "quitting sugar" journey for a few months and had successfully given up the white, sweet stuff. Desserts, cookies, and packaged foods were no longer part of my diet but were resulting in a very slow weight loss. I started this journey to lose weight, and to reverse metabolic syndrome, fatty liver, insulin resistance, and if I was very lucky, sleep apnea.

I was complaining about the slow loss to a friend, and she asked me if I was familiar with IF and the keto diet. I had never heard of it or of the keto way of eating. On that day, January 13, 2017, I came home and scoured the internvet for info. The first source of information was your wonderful website. I spent ALL weekend on your website just soaking it all in. I truly appreciate all the educational videos and testimonials. January 13, 2017, was the last day I ate potatoes, bread, and pasta. Those were the final high-carb foods that I kicked to the curb – and as a result, I had excellent results with weight loss. Because I had already quit sugar, there was little difficulty or withdrawal – I'm pretty sure I entered a ketosis state within a week of ditching those high-starchy carbs.

Nine months on the Keto and IF journey, I have dropped over 80 lbs. (36 kg) and am so very close to a healthy weight. I have also lost: daily headaches, monthly migraines, cystic acne, ovarian cysts, lethargic afternoons and evenings, joint pain, inflammation, and best of all sleep apnea – I no longer have to use a CPAP machine (confirmed with another sleep test that my obstructive sleep apnea is gone!). I have gained: a renewed joy for life, more energy than I know what to do with, a new appreciation for real food and cooking, shopping in regular size shops, improved self-esteem that has allowed me to be willing to put myself out there in ways I never dreamed of, and a sincere passion to share this way of life with anyone who asks me!

Turning 50 has been the best thing that has ever happened to me because it really lit a fire in caring for my personal health. My biggest challenge was letting go of potato chips – but repeating a question to myself as to what those (and other carby foods) would do to my insulin response, I was able to break that addiction and have no desire for those foods that obviously make me sick.

My biggest regret is not knowing about this way of life earlier, but I truly believe God's hand was in this journey with me every step of the way – making it easy to adopt this new lifestyle to stick with it 100%. I am so very grateful for real food and your website – it has truly given me the gift of LIFE to enjoy with my family and friends for many years to come. Here's to the next 50 years! God bless you and your work!

Sincerely,

Jane

Another one called Brad had this to say:

I did not realize how bad my life and health were until I got healthy. I am a 46-year-old from Vancouver Canada, a married father of a 10-year-old son.

I can make so many excuses why I got so large – usual story, former athlete, tore my ACL, became sedentary and lazy, finishing food off my sons' plate when he didn't finish his dinners. I ballooned up to 310 pounds (140 kilos), sleep apnea, high blood pressure, high cholesterol, lots of inflammation, and joint pain.

Started doing keto on May 12, 2018. I had listened to a few people who were talking about keto and intermittent fasting. So I read up on it and started the next day. I didn't wait and plan. My personality is to do it now, or something will pop up as an excuse.

It was easy to plan the first couple of meals because I had salad, veggies, and meats in the fridge. I'll also make low-carb protein shakes. Here in Canada, there is a brand that has 0.5 g carbs per serving. I'll add a tablespoon of roasted organic almond butter to that to increase my fat intake (and a nice flavor), and add unsweetened almond milk. Results were pretty good; two weeks in, I could feel clothes a bit looser, and the scale had moved downwards by 10 pounds (4.5 kilos). I was expecting the scale to move due to water loss.

I started walking my son to school instead of driving, and I would keep walking to the gym. I would do 20 minutes of stationary bike for the first week, then added some weights selecting a body part and do that for about 20 minutes, then would walk home. That was four times a week. Now, I do 37 minutes on elliptical and a good 45-minute workout. This is sandwiched between a 2-mile walk in each direction.

I started intermittent fasting about two and a half to three weeks in, as I was feeling pretty full on the higher fats of the foods I was eating anyway. Again, I heard people talk about it on the Joe Rogan podcast, so I started 16:8 for a bit, then gradually found 20:4 was good for me. Now I'm a big fan of OMAD (one meal a day). I'm basically OMD

Sunday-Wednesday, then I'll fast on Wednesday at 5 pm until Saturday at 5 pm. My aim is 22-hour fasts on OMAD but won't beat myself up on time. It's all about habits, and the gym is a habit or routine for me. I've been very, very strict. Have been fat-adapted from the start. I'm not eating (much) dairy and haven't played around with those fat bomb recipes I see everywhere.

During my time-restricted feeding, I will have coffee with heavy cream or black. If I get Starbucks, I'll order an Americano with heavy cream and add stevia. I'll have Zevia-carbonated water from time to time, but I was never a big cola drinker (I was into energy drinks, which was worse). I have made instant pot bone broth and enjoyed that as well. My main thing is that I drink a lot of water. I'll fill my 750-ml bottle endless times. Sometimes I'll add stevia. I know some will say I break the fast if I have coffee or Zevia, but this is about weight loss, and it's working for me. Keeps me on track. I'll do one seven-day true water fast once a quarter to for autophagy.

I'm down from a size 46 jeans to a 30/32, depending on style and cut and weigh about 170 pounds (77 kilos) down from 310 (140). I think 170-175 pounds (77-79 kilos) is my sweet spot, as I've played around from 165-175 (74-79). Just feel a bit stronger at 175 than 165.

My plan is to continue eliminating sugars and carbs out of my diet.

In summary, this is what has worked for me. I truly believe if I can do it, so can anyone. I have traded in my sugar addiction for an addiction to knowledge and research. I take in so many informative podcasts.

The keto combo with IF has been great, that's 80% of the battle. The other 20% comes from moving around. Even if it's just long walking. I started parking my car at the farthest spot possible. My steps increased from 3,000 a day to 15,000 now.

I have had a couple of nights where I have gone for wings and had some booze. I had either a low-carb beer or vodka soda. One night we went and had regular beer and ciders at a beer festival, and I didn't beat myself up about it, it was fun and worth it. I fasted for 24 hours, ate keto, and was back in ketosis right away. But that was two months into my journey, so I was fat adapted.

As far as supplements I take, I'll take a shot of apple cider vinegar at night and in the morning, and a tablespoon of MCT oil. Yes, I'll do them straight up. Other supplements: creatine before a workout, vitamin D3, a magnesium electrolyte supplement, and a fish oil capsule, and CoQ10, all in my feeding windows. I am now looking into supplementing with NMN (Nicotinamide Mononucleotide). Hopefully a Diet Doctor podcast article soon about that.

I am no longer on blood pressure medication, do not snore or have sleep apnea any more, and as of this month, my doctor allowed me to come off my statin RX. LDL was a bit high at 4.5 mmol/L, but I was at an optimal 3.5 ratio with HDL at 1.92.

So many excuses as to why I got huge to start with (ACL surgery, finish kids meals, not active, etc.) but don't look at the how did I get here, look at the how do I get OUT of here.

I receive text messages, and all are from friends and co-workers wanting help. I take as much pride in their success as I have had on my own. They want me to start my own blog, and even my doctor wants me to speak at conferences he goes to and shows off my biomarkers. My urine ACR (Albumin/Creatinine Ratio) was a dangerous high 112.6 and is now 2.0 after going keto and losing 145 pounds (65 kilos).

One of the mitigating factors when deciding to change things, was my sister who is a type 1 diabetic and needed a kidney transplant. It was determined that I was NOT a viable donor due to the bio markings of protein in my urine. They said if things kept going the way they were, I was going to need all my organs. I felt terrible that I could not donate my kidney to her. Fortunately, an amazing cousin was a match for her.

My life now is pretty amazing. I get inspired when people say that I inspire them. Considering how fast everything happened — a lot of people saw me six months ago, and see me today — they are shocked.

My weight loss was super fast. Thirty pounds (14 kilos) in the first 30 days, 90 pounds (49 kilos) in the first 60 days. Then the remaining 50 pounds (23 kilos) over the next four months. That's 145 pounds (65 kilos) in seven months. My goal was always 170 pounds (77 kilos).

Not sure why I set such a lofty goal, I think I just put in perspective of being a huge MMA (mixed martial arts) fan and figured Welterweight was the right weight class for me. Seemed unrealistic at first, but I wanted the goal really far away, so I would not stop short of my potential.

The biggest challenge was just starting it. Once I was determined to change my life, I was off to the races. I would go for high-sugar Starbucks drinks a couple of times a day; once I found an alternative (americano), I knew I could do this. I missed sushi, but I will have a poke bowl with a bed of salad instead of rice, add some good spicy fermented veggies like kimchi, I didn't miss sushi at all!

I wish I knew how much I could use avocados!! I smash my avocados into guacamole and add that to so many things. I'm fortunate enough that I make all the meals in the house five out of the seven nights, the other two I work in the evening, so I have 100% control my food intake.

My family hasn't complained at all about the great meals I am finding. I'll still cook them up homemade burgers, but I eat mine on a lettuce wrap, or cook up tacos, again in a lettuce wrap. It's pretty easy, and when the weight comes off quick, it's easy to stay motivated.

Thank you!

Brad

There are so many other success stories of people of different ages and sizes all around the world. You can do it! Even if you do not believe in yourself, I believe in you! All it takes is determination and patients. Anyone can do it!

Keto and
Intermittent Fasting

Date : ..../......./.......

Chapter 7

AFFORDABLE AND SIMPLE RECIPES

Keto and Intermittent Fasting

BREAKFAST RECIPES

CREAM CHEESE PANCAKE

PREPARATION
3 min

COOKING
9 min

SERVING
1

INGREDIENTS

- Cream cheese 2 ounces
- 1 tablespoon of coconut flour
- 1/2 teaspoon of cinnamon
- 1/2 to 1 pack of stevia
- 2 eggs

DIRECTIONS

1. Mix all ingredients until smooth and rest for two minutes
2. Heat the butter or coconut oil on a non-stick pan over medium-high heat
3. Make the pancakes just as ordinary pancakes would be
4. Cook for two minutes until golden brown then flip and cook for one minute more
5. Top with butter and/or sugar-free maple syrup and fresh berries

SPICED LATTE

PREPARATION
5 min

COOKING
2 min

SERVING
1

INGREDIENTS

- 2 cups of coffee
- 1 cup of coconut milk
- 1/4 cup Pumpkin Puree
- 2 teaspoon Pumpkin Pie Spice Blend
- 1/2 teaspoon Cinnamon
- 1 teaspoon Vanilla Extract
- 2 tablespoon Heavy Whipping Cream
- 2 tablespoon Butter, 15 drops Liquid Stevia

DIRECTIONS

1. Over medium-low heat, cook pumpkin, milk, butter Top with whipped cream and enjoy.
2. Froth the low carb pumpkin spice latte.
3. Add vanilla and use a milk frother to blend for about 30 seconds.

TIPS: The fastest and minimal-cleanup method is to heat right in the mug, in the microwave.

CAULIFLOWER WAFFLES

PREPARATION
5 min

COOKING
10 min

SERVING
3

INGREDIENTS

- 2 cup Raw Cauliflower
- 1 cup grated Mozzarella Cheese
- 1/2 cup Parmesan Cheese
- 1/2 cup Cheddar Cheese
- 2 Large Eggs
- 1/2 teaspoon Onion Powder
- 1/2 teaspoon Garlic Powder
- 1/4 teaspoon Red Pepper Flakes
- Pink Himalayan Salt and Pepper to taste

DIRECTIONS

1. Reduce cauliflower to flowers, with your food processor grate the flowers, once grated, squeeze the cauliflower in a kitchen towel, to make it as dry as possible

2. In a bowl, add grated cheese to the cauliflower

3. Add eggs and spices and blend all.

4. Cook and flip into a waffle maker 1/2 of the mixture. Repeat with the rest of the blend and remove from the waffle maker.

5. Top up with butter if you like it, otherwise they are also delicious like that.

TIPS: you can do this recipe by using purple cauliflower, top with two slices of crispy bacon and sour cream

BACON CHEDDAR EGG PUFFS

PREPARATION
7 min

COOKING
25 min

SERVING
12

INGREDIENTS

- 6 eggs
- 6 egg whites
- 6 slices of bacon, cooked and crumbled
- 3 ounces shredded cheddar cheese
- Salt and pepper to taste
- ¼ cup macadamia nuts

DIRECTIONS

1. Preheat oven to 350 F
2. Spray a muffin tin with nonstick cooking spray and set aside
3. In a bowl, beat egg and egg whites until well combined, season with salt and pepper to taste. Add crumbled bacon to the mixture, stir until mixed well
4. Pour egg mixture in the muffin tin, top each muffin with shredded cheese
5. Bake in the preheated oven for about 20-30 minutes until set

TIPS: enjoy half of your puffs with the macadamia nuts, use the rest of you puffs for another meal

EGG PORRIDGE

PREPARATION
3 min

COOKING
5 min

SERVING
1

INGREDIENTS

- 2 organic free-range eggs
- 1/3 cup organic heavy cream without food additives
- ½ teaspoon of stevia
- 2 tablespoons of grass-fed butter
- cinnamon to taste

DIRECTIONS

1. Add eggs, cream, sweetener in a bowl and whisk ingredients together
2. Melt butter over medium-high heat in a medium saucepan. Once the butter has melted, reduce the heat to a minimum.
3. Add the eggs and the cream mixture.
4. Cook, continuously stirring until the blend thickens and begins to curdle.
5. When you see the first signs of curdling, remove the pan from the heat instantly.
6. Pour in a bowl, sprinkle with cinnamon and serve right away.
7. Enjoy it!

TIPS: serve with fresh berries

EGGS FLORENTINE

PREPARATION

3 min

COOKING

4 min

SERVING

1

INGREDIENTS

- 1 cup washed, fresh spinach leaves
- 2 tablespoons of fresh parmesan cheese
- sea salt, and pepper to taste
- 2 teas
- poon of vinegar
- 2 eggs
- 1 tablespoon olive oil
- chili flakes to taste

DIRECTIONS

1. Toss the spinach in a nonstick pan with the olive oil on high heat until soft

2. Sprinkle with parmesan cheese, chili flakes and season to taste.

3. Lay everything in a serving plate

4. Set a pot full of water and vinegar to soft boiling, add salt and stir to create a whirlpool with a wooden spoon.

5. Break the egg in a small cup, then pour in the middle of the whirlpool and lower the heat while cooking it for 3-4 minutes, make sure that the whirlpool doesn't stop.

6. Repeat the same for the second egg.

7. Place and serve the eggs on the spinach

8. Enjoy it!

BULLET PROOF COFFEE

PREPARATION
Depends on your
coffee machine

COOKING
1 min

SERVING
1

INGREDIENTS

- 2 cups of hot brewed coffee
- 1 tablespoon of coconut oil
- 1 tablespoon of grass-fed butter or ghee

DIRECTIONS

1. Combine all ingredients in a blender, mix until frothy, enjoy immediately!

2. Note: bullet proof coffee doesn't work well iced, it will cause coconut oil to solidify

TIPS: to bring out the best from this recipe, use pure C8 MCT OIL, to add extra flavours, you can use either cinnamon on top, or unsweetened cocoa powder blended together.

SPINACH FETA MUFFINS

PREPARATION
5 min

COOKING
25 min

SERVING
6

INGREDIENTS

- 6 eggs
- 3 slices of bacon
- 2 cups of raw spinach
- 1 cup of crumbled feta cheese
- 1/2 cup of cheddar cheese
- salt and pepper to taste

DIRECTIONS

1. Wash, drain and microwave the spinach on top heat for 1 minute.
2. Set aside to cool down.
3. Cook bacon until you like.
4. Set aside to cool down.
5. Beat the eggs in a medium mixing bowl until smooth.
6. Mix the cheddar cheese with the crumbled feta cheese.
7. As quickly as the spinach and bacon are sufficiently cooled, add them to the eggs and then add the cheese.
8. Split the mixture into 6 cups of muffin evenly.
9. Bake at 350F for 15-20 minutes until the muffins are firm.
10. Enjoy it!

ALMOND PANCAKES

PREPARATION
4 min

COOKING
6 min

SERVING
8

INGREDIENTS

- ½ cup almond flower
- ½ cup cream cheese
- 4 eggs
- Cinnamon to taste
- Truvia to taste/vanilla extract
- Sides:
- 3 eggs
- Sea salt and pepper to taste
- 1 tablespoon grass-fed butter
- ¼ cup sugar free syrup

DIRECTIONS

1. Mix all ingredients in a blender until smooth

2. Spray griddle with a nonstick cooking spray. Over medium heat divide batter in 8 small pancakes. Allow to cook until middle begins to bubble 2-4 minutes, the flip and cook for another few minutes

3. Spray nonstick cooking spray in a medium pan, fry remaining 3 eggs, season with salt and pepper, cook to desire doneness

4. Enjoy your pancakes (2 pancakes are enough for a meal) with butter, syrup and eggs on the side.

TIPS: if you like, add some crunchy bacon

KETO BREAD

PREPARATION
6 min

COOKING
50 min

SERVING
6

INGREDIENTS

- 5 tablespoons of psyllium husk powder
- 1 ¼ cups almond flour
- 2 teaspoon baking powder
- 1 teaspoon sea salt
- 1 cup water
- 2 teaspoon cider vinegar
- 3 egg whites
- 2 tablespoon sesame seed if desired

DIRECTIONS

1. Preheat oven to 350 F
2. In a bowl mix all the dry ingredients
3. Bring the water to boil
4. Add vinegar and egg whites to the dry ingredients and combine well, add boiling water and mix for 30 seconds until you have the consistency of play-doh
5. Shape 6 rolls and put on the oven tray, top with sesame seeds if desired
6. Bake on lower rack for about 50-60 minutes
7. Serve with butter or toppings of your choice

Keto and Intermittent Fasting

LUNCH RECIPES

TUNA SALAD

PREPARATION

8 min

COOKING

5 min

SERVING

2

INGREDIENTS

- 2 cups of mixed greens
- 1 large tomato
- 1/4 cup of fresh parsley
- 1/4 cup of fresh mint chopped
- 10 large kalamata olives chopped
- 1 small zucchini chopped
- 1 1/2 avocado sliced longitudinally
- 1 cup of green onion
- 1 cup of tuna in olive oil
- 1 cup of extra virgin olive oil drained
- 1 cup of cider vinegar
- 1/4 Himalayan fine sea

DIRECTIONS

1. Cut the ingredients in bite dimensions.
2. In a big mixing bowl, add all the ingredients and mix well.
3. Enjoy it!

TIPS: to make the salad richer in protein, add some hard boiled eggs

JAMBALAYA

PREPARATION
30 min

COOKING
45 min

SERVING
6

INGREDIENTS

- 2 boneless skinless chicken breast halves
- 4 tablespoons olive oil, divided
- salt and freshly ground black pepper
- 2 tablespoons Cajun seasoning, preferably salt-free, divided
- 1 bag (16-ounce) cauliflower rice
- 1 large onion, finely chopped
- 2 stalks celery, chopped
- 1 red bell pepper, chopped
- 4 cloves garlic, minced
- 1 tablespoon Hungarian paprika
- 4 links Andouille sausage, halved lengthwise and sliced
- 1 can (15-ounce) petite diced tomatoes, undrained
- 8 ounces large peeled and deveined shrimp
- Tabasco sauce, to taste
- 1/4 cup chopped fresh parsley, divided

DIRECTIONS

1. Preheat oven to 375 degrees.
2. Place chicken breasts on a non-stick baking sheet. Drizzle with 1 tablespoon olive oil. Season evenly with salt, pepper and 2 teaspoons Cajun seasoning.
3. Bake for 22 - 25Place cauliflower on a non-stick baking sheet, drizzle with 1 tablespoon olive oil and season with salt, black pepper and 1 teaspoon Cajun seasoning.
4. Toss so that seasonings are evenly distributed. Roast for 10 minutes.
5. Meanwhile, heat remaining 2 tablespoons oil in a large skillet or sauté pan over medium-high heat.
6. Add the onion, reduce heat to medium and cook 4 - 5 minutes. Add the celery and red bell pepper and continue cooking another 7 - 8 minutes or until very soft. Keep heat at medium. Add the garlic, paprika, Andouille sausage and cook 2 minutes. Add tomatoes and shrimp and cook, stirring often until shrimp is cooked.
7. Cut the chicken into 1/2-inch pieces. Add to pan along with cauliflower and heat through.
8. Adjust seasonings and add tabasco sauce to taste. Add half the parsley.
9. Transfer to a serving platter and garnish with remaining parsley.

BUFFALO CHICKEN SOUP

PREPARATION

10 min

COOKING

30 min

SERVING

8

INGREDIENTS

- 1 tbsp olive oil
- 1/2 yellow onion about 1 cup diced
- 4 cups chicken broth
- 2-3 chicken breasts at least 1 lb. total
- 2 cup riced cauliflower about 1/2 head
- 1 can coconut milk
- 1 5 oz keto buffalo sauce
- 4 stalks of celery about 1 cup chopped
- 10 oz. cherry tomatoes
- 2 tbsp minced garlic
- 1 tsp dried dill
- 2 tsp paprika
- 1 tsp garlic powder
- 1/2 tbsp black pepper
- 1/4 cup fresh cilantro chopped
- 1/2 tsp pink hymalayan salt

DIRECTIONS

1. Begin by heating a large stock pot over medium heat with the olive oil
2. Dice the onion and add to pot. Allow to cook for 3-5 minutes, stirring occasionally until it becomes fragrant.
3. Add the broth and chicken breasts to the pot. As the chicken becomes more opaque flip it over.
4. Once the chicken has cooked, remove from the pot and set aside. While the chicken is cooking, rice the cauliflower if you have not done this already. To do so, remove the stalk from the head of cauliflower and cut into large chunks.
5. Throw half of the cauliflower into a food processor or blender and pulse until the cauliflower is in small bits.
6. Add to pot with the chicken.
7. Slice the celery thinly and add to pot once chicken is removed. Add the cherry tomatoes
8. Combine remaining ingredients into pot. Whisk together.
9. While coconut milk and spices heat, being shredding the chicken with a fork. Add chicken back to the pot and stir.
10. Serve immediately

JARLSBERG OMELET

PREPARATION
6 min

COOKING
10 min

SERVING
1

INGREDIENTS

- 4 medium sliced mushrooms
- 2 oz. 1 green onion
- 1 cup of butter sliced
- 2 eggs
- 1 oz Jarlsberg or Swiss cheese
- 2 slices of ham

DIRECTIONS

1. Cook the mushrooms the diced ham and the green onion in half of the butter in a big non-stick pan until the mushrooms are ready. Season with salt lightly, remove and set aside.

2. Melt over medium heat the remaining butter.

3. Add the beaten eggs

4. Now put the mushroom, ham and the grated cheese, on one side of the omelet.

5. Fold the plain side of the omelet over the filling once the eggs are almost ready.

6. Turn off the heat and leave until the cheese melts.

7. Enjoy it!

SHIITAKE AND PORK MEATBALLS

PREPARATION
20 min

COOKING
15 min

SERVING
6

INGREDIENTS

- 1 1/2 cups shiitake mushroom caps (about 4 oz.)
- 10 ounces pork tenderloin, cut into 1/2-in. pieces
- 1/2 teaspoon kosher salt
- 1/2 teaspoon black pepper
- 1 large egg, lightly beaten
- 2 tablespoons canola oil
- 1 bunch broccoli finely chopped
- 1 cup unsalted chicken stock
- cauliflower pearl from 1 cauliflower
- 1 tablespoon tamari soy sauce

DIRECTIONS

1. Place mushrooms and pork in a food processor; pulse 15 to 20 times or until finely chopped.

2. Place pork mixture in a bowl with 1/4 teaspoon salt, 1/4 teaspoon pepper, and egg; stir to combine.

3. Divide and shape pork mixture into 24 meatballs (about 1 tablespoon each).

4. Heat 1 1/2 teaspoons oil in a large skillet over medium-high.

5. Add Broccoli and cauliflower pearls; cook 4 minutes and set aside.

6. Add remaining 1 1/2 tablespoons oil to pan. Add meatballs; cook 5 minutes, turning to brown on all sides.

7. Combine 3/4 cup chicken stock with the tamari soy sauce, cover, reduce heat, and simmer 3 minutes or until meatballs are done.

8. Serve with the cauliflower and broccoli rice.

CROCKPOT SOUTHWESTERN PORK STEW

PREPARATION
10 min

COOKING
8 hours

SERVING
4

INGREDIENTS

- 1 teaspoon of paprika
- 1 teaspoon of oregano
- 1/4 teaspoon of cinnamon
- 2 Bay leaf
- 6 oz. button mushrooms
- 1/2 Jalapeno
- 1 lb. sliced cooked pork shoulder
- 2 teaspoons Chili Powder
- 2 teaspoons cumin
- 1 teaspoon minced garlic
- 1/2 teaspoon Salt
- 1/2 teaspoon Pepper
- 1/2 Onion
- 1/2 Green Bell Pepper, chopped
- 1/2 Red Bell Pepper, chopped
- Juice from 1/2 Lime
- 2 cups bone broth
- 2 cups Chicken Broth
- 1/2 cup Strong Coffee
- 1/4 cup Tomato Paste

DIRECTIONS

1. Cut vegetables and stir fry on high heat in a pan. Once done, remove from heat.

2. Put sliced pork into the crockpot, add the mushrooms, bone broth, chicken broth, and coffee.

3. Add all the seasoning with the sauteed vegetables and stir well.

4. Cover the crockpot and cook for 4-10 hours at low temperature.

This recipe can be done with a cast iron boiler, the cooking time will be around 1 hour 20 minutes

PAN-ROASTED RIB EYE STEAK WITH PAN JUS

PREPARATION
45 min

COOKING
20 min

SERVING
3

INGREDIENTS

- 1 (1 pound) rib-eye steak
- 4 spoons of olive oil
- 1/2 cup Chicken Broth
- 3 spoons of room temperature butter
- sea salt and pepper to taste

DIRECTIONS

1. Before cooking, remove steak from the fridge for about 45 minutes, pat it dry, and salt it completely. Flip it through for about 20 minutes, remembering when flipping to pat it dry, and then again before cooking.
2. If you want to cook your steak medium or medium-well, preheat your oven to 200 ° F. Heat on the stovetop a cast-iron skillet or another pan over elevated heat.
3. Add the oil to the casserole.
4. Place the meat in the pan just before it starts smoking, then listen to the searing sound.
5. Leave it to cook for 3 to 5 minutes without shifting it.
6. Once the bottom has a pleasant brown color (you can check by lifting one edge of the steak to look at the bottom) flip over the steak and do the same on the other.
7. This will offer you a steak that is medium-rare. If you want to continue cooking, place medium-well in the oven at 200 ° F for 5 to 6 minutes and medium-well for 7 to 8 minutes.
8. Once done, put it on a cutting board for 5 minutes to rest.
9. Slice it and serve it.
10. Make the pan jus while the meat rests.
11. Transfer the pan to the stovetop, add the broth and water over medium heat, reduce the sauce by half, add the butter and stir from 2 to 4 minutes.
12. Pour the Jus over the meat and enjoy.

MU SHU PORK

PREPARATION
15 min

COOKING
15 min

SERVING
6

INGREDIENTS

- 2 tablespoons avocado oil
- 2 tablespoons balsamic vinegar
- 1 tablespoon sesame oil
- 2 tablespoons coconut aminos
- 2 boneless skinless chicken breasts, thinly sliced
- ¼ green cabbage, thinly sliced
- ¼ red cabbage, thinly sliced
- ¼ cup green onions, sliced
- ½ cup mushrooms, chopped
- 2 cloves garlic, minced
- 1 teaspoon ginger, grated
- ½ teaspoon sea salt
- ½ teaspoon black pepper
- Carrots, shredded for garnishing
- Sprouts, for garnishing
- Sesame seeds for topping
- Butter lettuce for wraps

DIRECTIONS

1. In a medium-sized bowl, add sesame oil, balsamic, coconut aminos, ginger, garlic, salt, pepper and chicken. Mix thoroughly and set aside.

2. Chop the vegetables accordingly.

3. In a large pan over medium heat, combine avocado oil, onions and mushrooms. Sauté for about 5 minutes.

4. Add chicken to brown, about 8 minutes.

5. Add cabbage and reduce to low. Cover and let simmer for about 10 minutes, or until cabbage is soft. Stir occasionally.

6. Serve with lettuce wraps and top with carrots, sprouts and sesame seeds.

CHICKEN CURRY

PREPARATION
15 min

COOKING
40 min

SERVING
8

INGREDIENTS

- 1 small Onion roughly chopped
- 1 large Green Chili roughly chopped
- 1-inch Ginger roughly chopped
- 3 cloves Garlic
- 1/2 cup Cilantro leaves and stems
- 3 tablespoons grass fed butter
- 2 teaspoons turmeric ground
- 1 1/2 teaspoons cumin ground
- 1 teaspoon coriander ground
- 2 tablespoons tomato paste
- 2 pounds Chicken Thighs
- 1 cup Heavy Cream
- 1 teaspoon salt

DIRECTIONS

1. In your food processor, add the onion, green chili, ginger, garlic and fresh coriander.

2. Blend until all ingredients are finely chopped. If your food processor is struggling, add a tablespoon of water to help the ingredients move around.

3. Scrape the mixture out of the food processor and into a large saucepan over low heat, add the ghee and gently sauté for 10 minutes.

4. Add the turmeric, cumin and ground coriander and continue to gently sauté for another 5 minutes.

5. Add the tomato paste and stir well to combine with the other ingredients, continue to cook for another 2 minutes before adding the diced chicken.

6. Increase the heat to medium and cook the chicken in the spices for 10 minutes.

7. Add the cream and salt and reduce the heat until the curry is simmering.

8. Simmer for 20-25 minutes until the chicken is cooked through and the sauce has thickened.

9. Serve the Chicken Curry immediately with a side of Cauliflower Rice.

GARLIC SHRIMP

PREPARATION

25 min

COOKING

5 min

SERVING

2

INGREDIENTS

- 8 ounces uncooked big shrimp, peeled, deveined
- 1 teaspoon of coarse salt 1/4 cup of olive oil
- 1 tablespoon of sliced garlic
- 1 tiny bay leaf
- 1 teaspoon of crushed red pepper
- 1 lemon, zested and sliced into wedges
- 1 tablespoon of chopped parsley

DIRECTIONS

1. In a medium bowl, place the shrimp, sprinkle with coarse salt and set aside

2. Heat the oil over medium heat in a pan.

3. Stir in the garlic, bay leaf, and crushed red pepper for 1 minute.

4. Add shrimps to the pan, lay flat on one side to cook for 30 seconds to 1 minute, then twist the shrimps and fry for an extra 30 seconds.

5. Remove from heat, plate, sprinkle with lemon zest and parsley and enjoy!

QUICHE LORRAINE

PREPARATION
20 min

COOKING
45 min

SERVING
8

INGREDIENTS

Base:
- 2 cup almond flour
- 1 Egg
- 2 ounces grass fed butter
- 1 pinch salt
- 2 pinch white pepper

Filling:
- 4 slices diced bacon
- 1/2 Brown Onion diced
- 5 ounces gruyere cheese grated
- 3 eggs
- 1 1/2 cups whipping cream
- 1 teaspoon Dijon mustard
- 1 pinch salt
- 2 pinch white pepper

DIRECTIONS

Base:
1. Preheat fan forced oven to 170C/340F.
2. Mix the almond flour, salt, pepper, melted butter and egg.
3. Press the mixture into the base of your quiche dish and spread it evenly on the base and around the sides.
4. Bake the base for 12 minutes. If the base begins to rise from air bubbles, gently prick it with a fork and press the base back down.
5. Remove from the oven and set aside.

Filling:
1. Sauté the diced bacon and onion over medium heat until the onion is translucent.
2. Spread the bacon and onion mixture evenly over the base and top with the grated gruyere cheese.
3. In a large bowl or jug place the eggs, cream, mustard, salt, and pepper, blend together using a stick blender. Ensuring that all ingredients are well combined.
4. Gently pour the cream mixture over the bacon, onion and gruyere.
5. Place the quiche back in the oven and bake for 25 to 35 minutes, the quiche is ready when the centre no longer jiggles.
6. Remove from the oven and cut into 10 pieces. Enjoy.

TIPS: top your slice of quiche with your desired greens

CAULIFLOWER MUSHROOM RISOTTO

PREPARATION
10 min

COOKING
15 min

SERVING
6

INGREDIENTS

- 2 tbsp grass fed butter
- ½ large onion, finely diced
- 1lb portobello mushroom sliced
- 2 cloves garlic, minced
- 1 teaspoon fresh thyme
- 1 medium head cauliflower, riced
- ½ cup chicken broth
- ¾ cup heavy cream
- 1/3 cup grated parmesan cheese
- Salt and black pepper to taste

DIRECTIONS

1. Melt the butter in a sauté pan over medium heat.
2. Add the mushrooms and onions, and sauté for about 10 to 15 minutes, until the onions are translucent and browned, and the mushrooms are soft and browned.
3. The mushrooms should reduce in size by at least half, and no liquid should remain. (If needed, you can increase heat at the end to help evaporate the liquid.)
4. Add the minced garlic and thyme.
5. Sauté for about 1 minute, until fragrant.
6. Add the cauliflower and bone broth.
7. Increase heat to bring to a simmer, then simmer, stirring occasionally, until the cauliflower is tender, and liquid is reduced, about 3-5 minutes
8. Reduce heat to low.
9. Stir in the cream and Parmesan.

SPINACH SHAKE

PREPARATION
3 min

COOKING
–

SERVING
1

INGREDIENTS

- 1 ½ cup unsweetened almond milk
- ½ cup full fat coconut milk
- 1/3 medium size avocado
- 1 ½ scoops vanilla protein powder
- 1 ½ tablespoon macadamia butter
- 2 tablespoons flaked unsweetened coconut
- 4 cups raw spinach
- ½ tablespoon mct oil
- Dash of cinnamon
- 1-2 cups ice

DIRECTIONS

1. In a blender, combine all ingredients, blend until smooth and enjoy!

Keto and Intermittent Fasting

DINNER RECIPES

BAKED SPAGHETTI SQUASH

PREPARATION

15 min

COOKING

40 min

SERVING

8

INGREDIENTS

- 1 large spaghetti squash (about 3 ½ pounds),
- 3 teaspoons olive oil,
- 1 medium onion, chopped,
- 3 cloves garlic, finely chopped,
- 1 can (28 ounces) crushed tomatoes,
- 2 teaspoons dried Italian seasoning,
- ¼ teaspoon red pepper flakes,
- salt and black pepper to taste,
- 15 ounces ricotta cheese,
- 1 large egg,
- 5 ounces baby spinach steamed and chopped (can use frozen spinach),
- 2 cups shredded mozzarella cheese,
- 1/3 cup grated parmesan cheese,
- parsley for garnish.

DIRECTIONS

1. Preheat oven to 425°F.
2. Cut the squash in half lengthwise and remove the seeds.
3. Brush the flesh with 2 teaspoons oil.
4. Place them cut side down on a baking sheet lined with parchment paper.
5. Roast in the oven until tender, about 40 minutes.
6. Remove from oven and cool.
7. When the squash is cooled, scrape the flesh with a fork so that it forms spaghetti-like strands.
8. Meanwhile, make the sauce by heating 2 teaspoons oil in a large sauté pan over medium heat.
9. Add the onion and garlic and cook for 4 to 5 minutes until partially softened.
10. Stir in the tomatoes, Italian seasoning, red pepper flakes, ½ teaspoon salt, and ¼ teaspoon pepper.
11. Simmer the sauce until thickened.
12. Now, mix the ricotta, egg, spinach, 1 cup of the mozzarella cheese, salt and pepper together in a large bowl, squeeze all of the liquid from the spaghetti squash and add the squash to the ricotta mixture.
13. Turn the heat on the oven down to 375°F, now spread about 1½ cups of the sauce on the bottom of an 8 x 11-inch baking dish, add the squash mixture on top and spread it out evenly.
14. Spread the remaining tomato sauce over the top of the squash and sprinkle the remaining 1 cup mozzarella and parmesan cheese on top.
15. Bake in the oven until cheese is melted.
16. Garnish with parsley. Let stand for 10 minutes before cutting and serving.

BUFFALO PULLED CHICKEN AND BLUE CHEESE

PREPARATION
10 min

COOKING
40 min

SERVING
2

INGREDIENTS

- 1/2 a head of iceberg lettuce blue cheese dressing
- 2 tbsp crumbled blue cheese
- 4 slices of bacon
- 2 boneless chicken breasts
- 3/4 cup of sugar free buffalo sauce

DIRECTIONS

1. Bring a large pot of water to a boil and add some salt.
2. Add two chicken breasts to water and let cook for 30 minutes.
3. Once cooked, remove from water, and set chicken aside to cool for 10 minutes.
4. In the meantime, cook your four strips of bacon.
5. You want them well-cooked so that you can crumble them later.
6. Now cut the half iceberg lettuce, starting from the top towards the root, slice to make two wedges and plate up.
7. Now, using a fork, pull apart the chicken into small strips like you would pulled pork, heat up the buffalo sauce, add (if desired) a cube of butter, once hot, add the pulled chicken to the sauce.
8. Plate your chicken next to the lettuce wedges, then top with bleu cheese dressing, blue cheese and bacon crumbles. Enjoy!

CHICKEN CHORIZO

PREPARATION
5 min

COOKING
45 min

SERVING
4

INGREDIENTS

- 6–8 boneless skinless chicken breasts,
- 10-ounce chorizo,
- 4 ounces cream cheese,
- 1/2 Cup sour cream,
- 10-ounce chopped tomatoes with green chiles,
- 1/4 Cup freshly grated parmesan cheese

DIRECTIONS

1. Preheat the oven to 375 degrees.
2. Spray a 9×13 glass pan with nonstick spray.
3. Lay down the chicken evenly in the pan.
4. In a large pan, brown the chorizo over medium high heat for about 7-8 minutes, add the tomatoes, cream cheese and sour cream and mix well.
5. Pour the mixture over the chicken breasts, sprinkle on the parmesan cheese and bake for about 45 minutes depending on the size of your chicken breasts.
6. Enjoy!

MEATBALLS WITH ZUCCHINI NOODLES

PREPARATION

20 min

COOKING

30 min

SERVING

6

INGREDIENTS

MEATBALLS:
- 1 lb ground beef,
- 1/3 cup almond flour,
- 1/2 cup grated parmesan cheese,
- 1/4 cup shredded mozzarella cheese,
- 1/2 tsp garlic powder,
- 1/2 tsp onion powder,
- 1/2 tbsp Italian seasoning,
- 1 large egg

MARINARA SAUCE:
- 28 oz can dice tomatoes,
- 1/4 cup extra virgin olive oil,

- 1/4 tsp black pepper,
- 1 tsp onion powder,
- 1 tsp garlic powder,
- 1 tsp dried basil,
- 1 tsp dried oregano,
- 1 tsp dried parsley,
- 1 tsp salt

ZUCCHINI NOODLES:
- 1 ½ tbsp olive oil,
- 2 minced garlic cloves,
- 5 medium zucchinis already spiralized,
- salt.

DIRECTIONS

1. Preheat oven to 375F.
2. Line a large baking sheet with parchment paper.
3. In a large bowl, add all meatball ingredients.
4. Mix until everything is evenly blended.
5. Using a 1.5 tbsp scoop, scoop up meat and form into round balls.
6. Place onto prepared baking sheet.
7. You should be able to make about 25 meatballs.
8. Bake for 18-20 minutes or until meatballs are fully cook.
9. Now the sauce, add all marinara sauce ingredients to a blender.
10. Blend on low speed until pureed.
11. Pour sauce into a saucepan. Bring to a simmer and cook until thickened.
12. You should have approximately 3 cups of sauce.
13. Time for the noodles,
14. Add oil and garlic to large skillet. Bring to medium high heat.
15. Once oil is heated, add in zucchini. Cook until zucchini is tender but still crisp. Add salt as needed. Drain water from zucchini noodles.
16. Pour the zucchini in the marinara sauce and mix gently
17. Top with your meatballs and some parmesan cheese. Enjoy!

CAULIFLOWER PIZZA

PREPARATION
15 min

COOKING
30 min

SERVING
8

INGREDIENTS

- 1/2 lb Cauliflower (florets only - about one large head)
- 1 cup shredded mozzarella cheese
- 1 ½ cup grated parmesan cheese
- 1 large egg
- ½ tablespoon Italian seasoning
- ½ teaspoon garlic powder

DIRECTIONS

1. Preheat the oven to 400 degrees F
2. Place a piece of parchment paper onto a pizza peel if you plan to use a pizza stone (recommended), or a pizza pan.
3. Pulse the cauliflower florets in a food processor until they are the consistency of rice, put the cauliflower rice in a bowl and cook 1 minute in the microwave oven.
4. Now, put the rice in a kitchen towel and squeeze the excess of water.
5. In a large bowl, mix the rice with the rest of the ingredients, and mix well.
6. Pour the mixture on an oven tray with the parchment paper, spread it out with wet hands or a spatula.
7. Bake in the middle section of your oven until the surface is golden brown.
8. Now comes the funny part, its time to top your pizza crust with your favourite toppings (for example, top with tomato sauce, mozzarella cheese and sliced pepperoni), bake for about 5 minutes, making sure that the cheese is really melted.
9. Serve and enjoy!

BACON AVOCADO EGG SALAD

PREPARATION
10 min

COOKING
—

SERVING
2

INGREDIENTS

- 5 hard- boiled eggs, chopped
- 4 cherry tomatoes, sliced
- 3 slices bacon, cooked and chopped
- ¾ medium avocado mashed
- 1 tablespoon olive oil mayo
- 1 romaine lettuce, chopped
- Paprika to taste
- Salt and pepper to taste

DIRECTIONS

Olive oil mayo:
1. 1 egg yolk
2. 1 tablespoon lemon juice
3. 1 tablespoon water
4. 1 teaspoon Dijon mustard
5. 1 cup olive oil
6. Salt to taste

1. Pour all ingredients in tall container, using a blender, process until the mayo starts to thicken.
2. In a bowl combine chopped eggs, bacon, mashed avocado, tomatoes, olive oil mayo, lettuce and seasonings.
3. Mix until well combined and enjoy!

CREAMY BRUSSEL SPROUTS WITH BACON

PREPARATION
10 min

COOKING
25 min

SERVING
2

INGREDIENTS

- 10 ounces bacon, cut into strips,
- 2 tablespoons butter,
- 2 pounds Brussel sprouts, washed, (trim bottoms and cut sprouts in half),
- salt and pepper to season,
- 5 garlic cloves finely chopped,
- 1 1/2 cups heavy cream,
- 1/3 cup fresh shredded mozzarella,
- 1/4 cup grated parmesan cheese

DIRECTIONS

1. Preheat oven to 375°F.
2. Fry the bacon in a large oven-safe skillet over medium heat until crispy and set aside.
3. In the same pan, melt the butter, then add the Brussels sprouts and season with salt and pepper, cook and stir for about 6 minutes, now add in the garlic and stir it.
4. Pour in the cream, reduce heat down to low and allow them to simmer until tender (another 3-4 minutes).
5. Add the bacon and stir well.
6. Top the sprouts with the mozzarella and parmesan cheeses.
7. Bake in the oven for about 15 minutes.
8. Top with fresh herbs and enjoy!

FLANK STEAK WITH BROCCOLI GRATIN

PREPARATION
15 min

COOKING
40 min

SERVING
4

INGREDIENTS

- 8 oz. broccoli,
- 8 oz. cauliflower,
- ½ cup heavy whipping cream,
- 4 oz. shredded cheese,
- 20 oz. flank steak,
- salt and pepper,
- 2 tbsp olive oil, for frying

Pepper sauce:
- 1½ cups heavy whipping cream,
- 1 tbsp tamari soy sauce

DIRECTIONS

1. Preheat oven to 400°F.
2. Butter an 8x8-inch baking dish.
3. Clean, trim, cut broccoli and cauliflower into florets, then boil them in salted water for about 5 minutes and set aside.
4. Pour heavy cream, half of the shredded cheese and salt to a saucepan over medium heat until the cheese is melted, pour it over the broccoli and cauliflower that are already in a baking dish, now add the rest of the cheese and bake in the oven for 20 minutes.
5. Season the meat on both sides with salt and pepper, fry it in a large pan on high heat for about 4-5 minutes per side.
6. Place the meat on a cutting board and let the meat rest for 10-15 minutes before slicing it.
7. Pour cream, soy sauce and pepper into the frying pan.
8. Bring to a boil and let the sauce simmer until it becomes creamy, now cut the meat into ½ inch slices, serve with the gratin and pepper sauce.

LEMON DILL TROUT

PREPARATION
5 min

COOKING
16 min

SERVING
2

INGREDIENTS

- 2 pounds of trout,
- 1 1/2 teaspoon salt,
- 1/4 teaspoon pepper,
- 1/2 cup butter,
- 2 tablespoons dill,
- 3 tablespoons of lemon juice

DIRECTIONS

1. Season the fish with salt and pepper, melt half of the butter in a pan on high heat.
2. Fry the fish 8 minutes on each side, once done, put it on the serving plate.
3. In the same pan, add the rest of the butter with dill and the lemon juice to create the sauce, pour it over the fish and enjoy.

STUFFED CHEESY CHOPS

PREPARATION
15 min

COOKING
50 min

SERVING
4

INGREDIENTS

- 4 Thick Cut Pork Chops (3.67 lbs, 2" thick),
- 3 Slices Bacon,
- 3 oz. Bleu Cheese,
- 3 oz. Feta Cheese,
- 2 oz Green Onion,
- 2 oz. Cream Cheese,
- salt, pepper and garlic powder to taste

DIRECTIONS

1. Cook the bacon in a pan, reserve the grease and set the bacon aside.
2. Mix the blue and feta cheeses in a bowl,
3. Add the bacon, green onions and the cream cheese and mix until combine
4. Slice open the nonfat side of the pork chops.
5. Stuff with the cheese and bacon mixture. Use a toothpick to close the gap.
6. Season the chops with salt, pepper and garlic powder, then, over high heat, with the bacon grease sear the pork chops for 2 minutes per side, now transfer the chops to a greased pan and cook at 350 degrees for 45 minutes or until at desired finish temperature.

SHEPHERD PIE WITH CAULIFLOWER MASH

PREPARATION
10 min

COOKING
30 min

SERVING
4

INGREDIENTS

- 1½ lbs cauliflower
- ½ cup sour cream
- 1 egg
- 3 oz. butter, melted
- ½ leek, finely chopped
- 5 oz. cheddar cheese, shredded
- salt and ground black pepper
- 1 ¾ lbs ground lamb or ground pork
- 2 tbsp Worcestershire sauce
- 2 tbsp tamari soy sauce
- ½ tbsp tabasco
- 1 tsp onion powder
- salt and pepper

DIRECTIONS

1. Preheat the oven to 400°F.
2. Clean and cut the cauliflower into small florets.
3. Cook in lightly salted water until soft. Drain thoroughly.
4. Mash the cauliflower with a hand mixer or food processor.
5. Mix in sour cream, egg, butter, leek and half of the cheese.
6. Season with salt and pepper.
7. Fry the ground meat in butter.
8. Add the sauces and the spices.
9. Spread the meat out in an ovenproof dish and cover with the cauliflower mash
10. Top with the rest of the cheese and maybe some extra butter.
11. Bake in the oven for 20 minutes or until it gets a nice golden color.

PULLED PORK

PREPARATION
5 min

COOKING
8 hours

SERVING
8

INGREDIENTS

- 3 pounds boneless pork shoulder
- 1 tablespoon parsley
- 2 teaspoons cumin
- 2 teaspoons garlic powder
- 2 teaspoons onion powder
- 2 teaspoons salt
- 2 teaspoons paprika
- ½ cup broth

DIRECTIONS

1. Add the pork shoulder to a large slow cooker.

2. In a small bowl, stir together the parsley, cumin, garlic powder, onion powder, salt, and paprika. Rub mixture into the pork being sure to coat all sides.

3. Pour the broth into the bottom of the slow cooker.

4. Cover slow cooker and cook on low for 8 hours or high for 4 hours. Pork is ready when it easily shreds with a fork.

5. Shred the pork and stir the meat into the juices in the bottom of the slow cooker.

6. Serve immediately or keep warm in the slow cooker until ready to eat.

Fats and Oil

- Butter Coconut oil
- Coconut butter
- Olive oil
- Olives
- Avocados
- Avocado oil
- Coconut flakes (unsweetened)
- Full-fat coconut milk
- Butter
- Sesame oil

Condiments and Spices

- White vinegar
- Apple cider vinegar
- Hot sauce
- Garlic powder
- Onion powder
- Chives
- Cinnamon
- Pumpkin puree
- Red pepper flakes
- Paprika
- Cajun seasoning
- Mayonnaise

Protein

- Poultry: chicken
  (free-range is best)
- Meat: beef, lamb, rib-eye steak
  (grass-fed is best)
- Pork: pork loin, ham, pork chops
  (humanely treated, pastured is best;
  make sure ham contains no sugar)
- Eggs
- Bacon
- Sausage
- Smoked sausage
- Fresh fish: salmon, mackerel, trout, tuna
- Shellfish: shrimp, crab, lobster, scallops, mussels, oysters, clams
- Canned tuna
- Canned salmon

Nuts, Nut Butters, and Seeds

- Nuts
- Macadamia
- Walnuts
- Almonds
- Sunflower seeds
- Pumpikin seeds

Dairy Products

- Heavy cream
- Sour cream
- Ricotta cheese
- Cottage cheese
- Cream cheese
- Cheddar cheese
- Parmesan cheese
- Pepper jack cheese
- Mozzarella cheese
- Bleu cheese
- Swiss cheese
- Crumbled feta cheese

Sweeteners and Extracts

- Stevia (liquid and granulated)
- Vanilla extract
- Sea salt
- Tomato paste

Others

- Coffee
- Tea bags

Vegetables

- Black peppers
- Spinach
- Baby kale
- Cabbage
- Cauliflower
- Lettuce
- Onions
- Garlic
- Mushrooms
- Celery
- Brussels sprouts
- Asparagus
- Zucchini
- Spaghetti squash
- Tomatoes
- Green pepper
- Mustard greens
- Carrots
- White beans
- Jalapenos
- Springs fresh flat-leaf parsley
- Thyme
- Bay leaf

Fruits

- Lemon

Chapter 8

30-DAY MEAL PLAN

Week 1

DAY	BREAKFAST	LUNCH	DINNER
1	Bullet Proof Coffee	Tuna Fish Salad	Pulled Pork
2	Bullet Proof Coffee	Buffalo Chicken Soup	Lemon Dill Trout
3	Bullet Proof Coffee	Cauliflower Mushroom Risotto	Flank Steak with Broccoli Gratin
4	Bullet Proof Coffee	Chicken Curry	Creamy Brussel Sprouts with Bacon
5	Bullet Proof Coffee	Garlic Shrimp	Cauliflower Pizza
6	Bullet Proof Coffee	Pan-Roasted Rib-Eye Steak with Pan Jus	Meatballs with Zucchini Noodles
7	Bullet Proof Coffee	Spinach Shake	Chicken Chorizo

Week 2

DAY	BREAKFAST	LUNCH	DINNER
1	Spiced Latte	Bacon Avocado Egg Salad	Pan-Roasted Rib-Eye Steak with Pan Jus
2	Bacon Cheddar Egg Puffs	Chicken Curry	Baked Spaghetti Squash
3	Egg Porridge	Quiche Lorraine	Stuffed Cheesy Chops
4	Spinach Feta Muffins	Garlic Shrimp	Shepherd Pie
5	Bullet Proof Coffee	Buffalo Chicken Soup	Lemon Dill Trout
6	Almond Pancakes	Garlic Shrimp	Cauliflower Pizza
7	Keto Bread with Favorite Topping	Shiitake Mushroom Pork Meatballs	Chicken Chorizo

Week 3

DAY	BREAKFAST	LUNCH	DINNER
1	Spinach Feta Muffins	Cauliflower Mushroom Risotto	Pulled Pork
2	Cauliflower Waffles	Chicken Curry	Flank Steak with Broccoli Gratin
3	Cream Cheese Pancake	Pan-Roasted Rib-Eye Steak with Pan Jus	Lemon Dill Trout
4	Bullet Proof Coffee	Tuna Fish Salad	Shepherds Pie with Cauliflower Mash
5	Bullet Proof Coffee	Shiitake Mushroom Pork Meatballs	Creamy Brussel Sprouts with Bacon
6	Bacon Cheddar Egg Puffs	Mu Shu Pork	Cauliflower Pizza
7	Egg Porridge	Buffalo Chicken Soup	Chicken Chorizo

Week 4

DAY	BREAKFAST	LUNCH	DINNER
1	Spinach Feta Muffins	Quiche Lorraine	Meatballs with Zucchini Noodles
2	Egg Florentine	Mu Shu Pork	Buffalo Pulled Chicken and Blue Cheese
3	Almond Pancakes	Jarlsberg Omelet	Baked Spaghetti Squash
4	Cauliflower Waffles	Tuna Fish Salad	Flank Steak with Broccoli Gratin
5	Bullet Proof Coffee	Quiche Lorraine	Creamy Brussel Sprouts with Bacon
6	Spinach Feta Muffins	Mu Shu Pork	Buffalo Pulled Chicken and Blue Cheese
7	Bullet Proof Coffee	Shiitake Mushroom Pork Meatballs	Meatballs with Zucchini Noodles

Chapter 9

Most Frequent Questions on Ketogenic Diet and Intermittent Fasting

Between eating vegetables raw and cooked, which is better?

There are a number of discussions on this matter. Some individuals claim that cooking kills vitamins, minerals, and enzymes, but as it softens cellulose strands, making it among other nutrients more accessible to the body. Tomatoes have a powerful oxidant that is stimulated when cooked. Other vegetables produce more antioxidants when prepared, including carrots, mushrooms, spinach, cabbage, and peppers; the downside is that vitamin C can be damaged when you prepare them. There's no official response, strive to consume plenty of vegetables in whatever manner you feel like.

Is it possible to eat anything during my feeding window during a fast?

This is correct because no foodstuff is prohibited. Fish, fries, bread, pizza, biscuit, and even burgers, everything and anything! Do not consume excessively in order to compensate for the period gone during the fast, as if you were in a contest. This can reverse the intended fasting outcome. It shouldn't be turned into a routine, where you fast then binge-eat; you should eat it in moderation. You can pig out, but why would you? By now, you understand the impacts of surplus meals in your body if you have been reading this book. After a while pursuing the regiment, you will discover that you will start choosing healthier meals out of your own accord.

Is there a distinction between distinct genders in reaction to intermittent fasting?

Hormonally and metabolically, men and females vary a lot. Women obviously have more fat and are more responsive to exercise-based fat burning and are good at fat preservation. Studies have been done that demonstrate that females who are fasting react faster to endurance training while males who are fasting have a stronger weight training reaction. Both genders enjoy nearly the same advantages. You should be more self-aware and focus on your fasting adventure, as fasting not intended to be a contest.

What if I don't lose weight?

There will be no immediate weight loss; it will take a while. If you don't lose weight in the first week, do not worry, just keep on going. If you're waiting and still don't lose weight, you should look at what you're eating as that's where the problem is most probably at. It's best to maintain a record of what you consume so you can monitor the matter.

Is fasting healthy to do when I'm on my period?

Fasting, as mentioned previously in this book, when you are pregnant or breastfeeding is not fine, but there is no justification not to fast on your period unless they are unpleasant or heavy. If they are, you should go and test your iron amounts and take supplements as well.

Can I be grumpy because of fasting?

In all its time it has been used, this has never been an issue in intermittent fasting. It is not even recognized as a problem by cultures that have fasting as an essential aspect of their convictions in all their years. Buddhist monks do seem to be basically fasting every day, but have you ever seen people saying that they are cranky? Fasting has no effect of this kind.

Is it ok to use meal substitute shakes to assist me to get through the first fasting days?

These meal replacement shakes have helped many individuals through the first weeks. They are certainly simpler to count than calories because you can just drink off your hunger. Even if it is thought that true eating is better if you discover that these shakes will assist you to use them. Remember to drink sugarless ones so as to keep you in ketosis

What weight am I going to lose while fasting?

This differs from individual to individual and relies on a number of variables. These variables are like your pace of metabolism, your level of exercise, and how honestly you are fast and diet. You may encounter water loss in the first week, which will cause a noticeable shift in the scales and with n due time the calorie deficit will result in you losing weight. Very quick weight loss is not recommended and should not be your goal; it is best to constantly lose a small quantity of weight a long period of time as it is easier to maintain.

Is it okay to refuse to take food in social settings since I'm on a fast, or that the food will pull me out from ketosis?

Be involved in your engagement, but you should be very engaged in what you take. Although support for family and friends is important if you make it a constant song about how you can't consume because of you are on a diet, it may reach a point that it will seem rude. Instead of something that should fit seamlessly in your lives, this will render your diet a life barrier. If you know there's a food-related social event, then fast the day before or the day after but make sure you do not eat to the point you are out of ketosis, just take small nibbles here and there so that you don't stand out. It's a very versatile regiment, so you can still join these activities and celebrate with them.

Will I feel exhausted as a result of intermittent fasting?

No, actually the reverse is going to occur. People usually discover that when fasting, they have more energy; this is most probably due to enhanced adrenaline levels. There is no doubt that you will have more than enough energy to perform ordinary daily operations. Fatigue is not a standard component of fasting, so you should stop fasting instantly and see a doctor if you feel excessively tired constantly.

Can fasting contribute to excess feeding?

Yes, it may because immediately after fasting, you'll consume more than normal. But the fasting period does not lead in food being consumed above the standard quantity on non-fasting days.

What am I going to do on days of fasting since I take my medication with food?

If you take them on an empty stomach, you may encounter certain side effects with certain medications. Iron supplements can trigger nausea and vomiting; aspirin can trigger ulcers and upsets in the stomach. It's best to ask your doctor if you should proceed to take this medicine when you're fasting. With small leafy vegetables that have low calorific values, you can take the medication together with them so it won't interrupt your speed. Your blood pressure may fall during fasting times, so if you take blood pressure-lowering medicine, your blood pressure may become too small and trigger headaches.

What if I'm overweight?

Intermittent fasting has demonstrated to be one of the most efficient and sustainable forms of losing and keeping off weight for obese individuals. In fact, your original weight loss is bigger, the bigger you are. You've most probably failed traditional restrictive diets. Intermittent fasting is good because it is more versatile, there is no guilt when you consume something as nothing is limited, and on your living window, it approves food for enjoyment. Studies have been carried out that demonstrate that obese individuals very quickly adopt intermittent fasting.

Naturally, I am a slender individual; can I still experience the intermittent fasting health advantages?

If you're already pleased with your weight, efficiently fasting is still feasible. You need to be sure that you concentrate more on calorie-dense products during the eating window. A lot of slender individuals fast for its health benefits you will get that sweet spot between eating and fasting after the trial and error, which will aid you to keep your weight at a manageable level. Reduce your days of fasting and watch the scale as well so that you don't end up becoming underweight.

Will I be able to sleep hungry?

It's unlikely, but depending on your metabolism and fasting timetable, it differs. Just try to keep your mind off it if you feel hungry. You may not feel hungry at all when you wake up. Eventually, your hunger and appetite will follow your timetable of fasting.

Can I eat snacks on a Keto diet?

Needless to say, high-carb products may not fit into the diet of keto. One cup of popcorn includes 5 g of carbs that can be a quarter of your full day's carb allowance. Also worth noting is that one cup of popcorn only includes about thirty calories and no fat, so it's not going to fill your belly. Approximately a quarter cup of simply dried oats has 12 grams of carbohydrates for 77 calories and only 1 gram of fat.

As far as yogurt is concerned, it varies on what sort of yogurt you choose and whether it complies with keto. Remember to choose plain variants as more sugar, and therefore carbs are added to the flavored ones. Better keto-compliant meals include beans, seeds and tiny quantities of low-carb fruits such as berries. Other nice snack choices on keto are beef jerky and non-starchy veggies like broccoli and cucumbers.

Do I have to worry about Keto Flu?

If you're keen on the keto diet, you've most likely heard about keto flu, a side effect that's not that fun. It is a real thing. Your body was structured so as to work on carbohydrates, and it does it really well. It becomes less energy efficient when it moves to fat burning you have less energy at your disposal on keto, and you may feel tired and sluggish as if you had the flu. You will pop out of it as your body adjusts naturally to this fresh manner of getting energy, but it can even take a few weeks.

Can my body get into starvation mode and hold on to fat?

This is not feasible because there is no limitation on calories. Your fasting is never going to be so intense that you reach starvation mode. This is because the duration of fasting is brief, so your body burns fat from fat stores and does not use muscle tissue. Research has shown that intermittent fasting does not suppress metabolism. There will be no reduction in the basal metabolic rate even during lengthy fasts like those for three days. It does not increase the hunger hormone concentrations called ghrelin either.

Can I get headaches during the fast?

It may occur, but only due to dehydration and not due to the absence of sufficient calories. You may encounter signs of withdrawal from sugar, but they are gentle. Make sure you are constantly taking water and cope with headache as you would a normal headache. If the day of fasting makes you feel sick, then you should stop immediately.

Do I have to think about low blood sugar?

Your body is a very effective device intended to regulate blood sugar

Your blood glucose concentrations should stay stable if you follow the rules in this book. If you are fasting for more than two times a week, it is suggested to use the 24-hour fast technique. Remember always to consult a doctor for any nutritional changes if you are diabetic.

If I want to get pregnant, is it ok to fast?

There has not been much study on this subject, but intermittent fasting has been shown to have no effect on fertility. Fertility can be affected by other intense types of fasting. If you're trying to get pregnant and once you're pregnant, fasting is completely off the table, to be on the healthy side of things.

What if I use a cookie to cheat my fasting period?

Intermittent fasting is a voluntary procedure involving abstinence from meals. Not just because you eat fewer calories that you lose weight, it's because it's what your body was built to do. The goal of intermittent fasting is to give your body a relaxing period free of food. During your fasting period, having only one additional cookie will slow your advancement and increase your blood sugar concentrations.

Is the ketogenic diet good?

The diet is popular, and it's been used by many to lose weight. However, eating elevated concentrations of saturated fat may present a threat to long-term cardiac health; and severe low carb diets may result in unpleasant side effects, such as constipation and headaches. Because of the rigid nature of keto, it eliminates most fruits and dairy, whole grains, many vegetables, and legumes, some nutrients, such as fiber.

Is it safe to follow the Keto diet?

Although it may feel like a radical manner to eat because of the exceptionally elevated fat diet; studies of ketosis through this diet have shown no true adverse effects when performed in a brief time. Ketosis is a natural metabolic state that causes keto to lead to weight loss. However, there have been few long-term trials of the diet. It's hard to tell that it's absolutely secure, and it also relies mainly on the kinds of food you eat on a diet. Olive oil, for example, is a healthier option than butter; salmon is healthier than bacon. That said, following a proper keto diet, and with the assistance of a medical practitioner, adverse health impacts should be reduced.

Is it bad to be in the ketosis state?

In normal conditions, carbohydrates are used by the body for energy. Ketosis is when your body has changed to a state of fat burning and turns fat into ketone bodies that are used as energy. Many trials have shown, that beyond keto flu, entering ketosis via diet has no true adverse short-term effects. Long-term research should be carried out to really evaluate the effect of the diet. It's probably not dangerous to put your body in ketosis for a finite duration.

What if I have diabetes?

If you have type 1 or form 2 diabetes or are taking diabetic medicines, extra care is required. Your doctor should monitor you carefully and track your blood sugar concentrations and modify your medication as needed. If you can't be closely monitored, then don't try to fast. It lowers blood sugar concentrations so ongoing diabetes medication such as insulin being taken as you fast, your blood sugar can become incredibly small, leading to very hazardous hypoglycemia. You can take some juice or sugar to increase your blood sugar concentrations; you can even take a day off to keep your blood sugar concentrations at good levels. If you have repeatedly low levels of blood sugar, it doesn't happen because of intermittent fasting; it's because you're over-medicated. Reduce your medication in anticipation of lower blood sugar concentrations before starting the fast.

Is it too late for me to start fasting?

There is no right time to start; if you have not started, you should because you don't have time to lose. Fasting can extend your life; it also moderates your appetite and helps you lose weight. You are going to experience the impacts fast; you are going to feel healthier, leaner, and more energy.

How long should I keep fasting?

This eating system is truly very similar to that of individuals who are slender by nature. They're going to consume some dishes and skip others according to how their bodies direct them, that's how the regiment is. As you become accustomed to the practice of choosing your calorie consumption, you will lower your calorie consumption until it becomes natural to you. You can alter the quantity of fasting you do once you reach your intended weight. You shouldn't stop fasting because it is intended to be a continuous shift in lifestyle, but not a temporary exercise. It's an ongoing practice that guarantees you've maintained your weight loss.

How much weight, on the Keto diet, can you lose?

It is proven that the diet can help boost weight loss, and it's simple to discover unscientific accounts of dramatic changes while on a diet. Many people have quite dramatic changes in the body. There is a test that was carried out was about 20 individuals with obesity that lived on a very low-calorie keto diet and lost an average of 44 pounds mostly from the body and visceral fat in four months. People with regular weight following a calorie-restricted keto diet lost about 4 lbs. in both fat and lean body mass in six weeks. But long-term trials indicate that between keto and other diets there is not much distinction in weight loss. A comparison of adults with some on a standard low-fat diet and some on a ketogenic diet was carried out. Those on the keto diet dropped two more pounds than to those that cut fat consumption after at least a year. Diets can aid you to lose the same quantity of weight in a long term basis. Know that with that, you may select another option of the diet without a lot of doubts.

How could the diet of Keto affect my period?

There is a chance that you might see a menstrual shift. Studies on young females eating severe low-carbs over a long duration eventually face irregular periods or even miss them at times. This effect can also come about as a result of rapid weight loss. Severely restricting carbohydrates can affect the adrenal system, resulting in hormonal imbalances that interfere with the menstrual cycle of a woman. So women may need more carbs as opposed to males on a keto diet, particularly if a female notices a shift in her menstrual cycle.

On the other hand, there is limited proof that a ketogenic diet for females can enhance their hormonal equilibrium. A tiny number of females who underwent a 24-week keto diet lost 12% of their body weight and decreased testosterone and insulin levels. Talk to your doctor, particularly if you use the diet as part of your therapy.

How long do you need to lose weight on the Keto diet?

Many individuals report weight loss on a keto diet rapidly. There was a study taken where the dieting group was obese, and they lost an average of about 20 KG over four months. Many people do not spend more than three months in ketosis due to long-term follow-up uncertainties and the danger of nutritional deficiencies emerging.

When individuals go off a keto diet and start incorporating more carbs into their daily intake, they tend to regain some weight during this adaptation phase. They also begin to regain all the weight they have lost and possibly more if they return to their pre-keto eating methods, thus feeling they wasted time on the scheme.

Can Type 2 Diabetes be reversed by the keto diet?

While this is not the first instrument, you should use to for you to regulate your insulin, carb counting and uniformly spreading carbs throughout the day, can be simpler to stick to.

Some studies indicate that keto may be a useful strategy for some individuals with type 2 diabetes. There was a study taken where overweight adults with type 2 diabetes were put in two groups, one of which followed the ketogenic diet, and the other ate a low-fat diet. The keto team saw their average blood sugar over a three-month period drop more than the control group after seven months to less than 6.5 percent. The keto group also dropped 12 KG and the control group about 3 KG.

But there is a need for long-term research, and keto can present health hazards to individuals with diabetes, particularly if you follow it without professional medical oversight. Importantly, anyone who is on medication to decrease blood sugar or who uses insulin should be conscious that, as you must do on keto, drastically reducing carbs can contribute to extremely low blood sugar. Unaddressed, this disease, known as hypoglycemia, may result in seizures, loss of consciousness, and make your vision blurred. Individuals with type 1 diabetes are not supposed to attempt the keto diet. If you have type 2 diabetes, be sure to operate with your doctor, and handle your aspirations. Not only is there no conclusion as to whether the keto is effective in dealing with diabetes, but it's also hard to stick to it. Keep in mind that type 2 diabetes cannot be corrected, but it can be placed into remission.

Keto and
Intermittent Fasting

Conclusion

Your dedication to improve your health and lose weight is phenomenal since you have been able to reach the end of this book. It is not an easy process to lose weight if you will be able to maintain the guidelines you have learned in this book and stay motivated; your life will change in ways that you cannot imagine. You are on the right track to achieve both mental and physical health. Even though adjusting to eating a healthy diet after being accustomed to eating a lot of convenience foods is a challenge you will feel the difference in energy levels that you will experience. You will look good and be safe from many of the common nutrition-related diseases and conditions and on top of all of that; your quality of life will improve greatly.

We are all different thus you should take time to really understand what a weight loss program involves and try out the program gradually. If you nose dive into a weight loss program is not advisable since it may not be for you. No regiment works perfectly for everyone thus you should select a plan and modify it in a way that suits you. There are many weight loss programs with mind-blowing results but they may be too hard to follow or just unsafe to practice.

In order to select an intermittent fasting regiment, you should consider the activities happening in your life. You work out intensity, duration, your resting period are all factors that should be considered. It best works when it is a constant in your daily activity and as it is not a permanent change of your physical and psychological condition.

In order to get the maximum weight loss experience, you should listen to your body. This does not mean that you should eat any time you feel hungry, it means that you should listen to how it responds to your diet and fasting regiment because the body system determines the time for you to eat, time for you to exercise and even how many calories you take in. Thus you will be in full control of your weight loss once you are in control of your diet and fasting program.

You should know that even though the ketogenic diet is about carbohydrate restriction, do not excessively restrict them you should make sure you eat enough. If you restrict calories too much you will be moody and it can even stop your fat loss process. You should also vary your food choices so that you make sure that you are getting the nutrients you need so as to maintain your health.

In fact, getting all the nutrients that you require from a ketogenic diet is possible. Unfortunately for some, this is not possible. If you do not feel okay, you should go and see a doctor so as to determine if you have any nutritional deficiencies. He/she will able to recommend supplements for you from that information.

You may want your weight to melt off like an ice cube in the summer but this is not advisable. We are naturally impatient; this makes people jump from one regiment to another as the one they were on did not produce results fast enough. For health reasons, weight loss should be a slow process. Losing 2 pounds a day is okay, but anything more than that is a lot. Engage in your day-to-day operations while fasting as this is a time-flying route. Being idle will certainly hold your mind centered on m we've come to the book's end.

There is some very important thing is that you should always try to do so as to get maximum weight loss. Always begin each morning with a full eight-ounce glass of water. It will help you start your day hydrated and set the tone for drinking plenty of fluids throughout the day. Always try to be busy so as to keep your mind off the food you should fast on a busy workday you will realize that you will be too busy to be hungry. Make sure that you drink coffee since it is a mild appetite suppressant. There's also some evidence that green tea may suppress appetite. Black tea and homemade bone broth may also help control appetite. Remember that hunger comes in waves and is not constant. Slowly drink a glass of water or some coffee once you start feeling hungry. Often by the time you've finished, your hunger will have passed. You shouldn't inform people that you are fasting. This is because most people will try to discourage you as they don't know or understand the benefits of fasting. Having a small group of people who are fasting is better than telling people who are not fasting as they know the importance of fasting and its challenges. It takes time but your body eventually adapts to the new conditions. As stated before, starting these regiments will be challenging but you should keep on going. On none fasting days, you should eat a nutritious diet. Intermittent fasting is not an excuse to eat whatever you like. During non-fasting days, try to stick to a nutritious diet low in sugar and refined carbohydrates. Following a low-carbohydrate diet that's high in healthy fats can also help your body stay in a fat-burning mode and make fasting easier. Avoid binge eating then after your fast, pretend that it never happened. Eat normally, as if you had never fasted. Fasting should fit in your life.

I hope this book gives you sufficient data on weight loss through intermittent fasting and the ketogenic diet and the steps you need to take to start your weight loss journey. The sky is the limit; you can achieve all your body and health goals just as long as you are persistent and ready to deny yourself now for a better tomorrow. Good luck in your weight loss journey and have a fun time doing it.

Keto and
Intermittent Fasting

Printed in Great Britain
by Amazon